you&your

Land Rover Ninety, One Ten &

Defender

you & your

Land Rover Ninety, One Ten &

Defender

BUYING, ENJOYING, MAINTAINING, MODIFYING   MARTIN HODDER

© Martin Hodder 2000

Martin Hodder has asserted his right to
be identified as the author of this work.

First published in November 2000

British Library cataloguing-in-publication data:
A catalogue record for this book is available from
the British Library.

Published by Haynes Publishing,
Sparkford, Nr Yeovil, Somerset BA22 7JJ
Tel: 01963 442030 Fax: 01963 440001
Int. tel: +44 1963 442030 Fax: +44 1963 440001
E-mail: sales@haynes-manuals.co.uk
Web site: www.haynes.co.uk

ISBN 1 85960 667 9

Library of Congress catalog card number 00-134245

Haynes North America Inc.
861 Lawrence Drive, Newbury Park,
California 91320, USA

Designed and typeset by G&M,
Raunds, Northamptonshire

Printed and bound by in Great Britain by
J.H. Haynes & Co. Ltd, Sparkford

Note on imperial/metric conversions

Unless usually referred to in metric units (eg engine capacity in
cubic centimetres [cc] or litres) or imperial units (eg carburettors
in inches [in]), common measurements are given in imperial units
with metric equivalents in parenthesis, except in the following
less common instances:

$282 \div$ miles per gallon (mpg) $=$ litres per 100 kilometres (l/100km)
Torque: pounds-force feet (lb/ft) x 0.113 $=$ Newton metres (Nm)
Pressure: pounds-force per square inch (psi) $=$ Kilopascals (kPa)

Contents

Acknowledgements

In writing this book I have drawn heavily on my own knowledge of Land Rovers and on information contained in the very large number of articles I have written about the vehicles in magazines such as *4-Wheel Drive*, *Motor*, *Classic Car Weekly*, *Popular Classics* and *Land Rover Owner*.

I have also cross-referenced my own inform-ation with other sources, and in this respect I must pay a special tribute to the excellent and numerous works by James Taylor. James is, without doubt, the greatest authority on Rover and Land Rover, and his books are used for reference by a great many writers, myself included. He and I now work alongside each other on Britain's newest Land Rover magazine, *Land Rover enthusiast*.

Most of the more historical photographs have been supplied by James, and the bulk of the rest have come from Nick Dimbleby. The more practical pictures were taken specially for the book by Dave Barker, another close friend and long-time colleague.

Further assistance has come from Richard Green, proprietor of the world's largest Land Rover bookshop, and from David Mitchell, David Bowyer, and Pete Wilford.

To all these people I owe a hearty 'Thank you', as I do to the very many experts and enthusiasts who, over the years, have willingly provided me with the information and advice which all journalists need in order to do their work.

Martin Hodder
Malaga
September 2000

Author Martin Hodder takes a break while enjoying an off-road outing in the Scottish Highlands with the late-1960s Land Rover Series IIA which he 'used and abused' for many years.

Introduction

There is nothing else in the world like the Land Rover Defender. No other motor manufacturer has been able to create a machine which combines the rainbow of qualities possessed by each of the models within the Defender family, and there's not another vehicle with the same fervent following.

Passion is something you would expect to be associated with Ferrari, not Land Rover, so why is it that anything from the Solihull factory attracts devotion which is the envy of all other car makers? Why have all Land Rovers been so revered for more than half a century? How is it that countless thousands would choose a Defender any day, rather than a sleek roadburner from Modena, Stuttgart or Munich?

The simple answer is that Defenders are no-nonsense, intensely honest vehicles which do everything asked of them without protest. They incorporate all that Land Rover has learned since 1948, and are the culmination of that experience, giving them off-roading capability without equal and on-road performance which, although definitely not in the supercar league, is well up to the job of daily commuting and long-distance holiday motoring.

Yet the appeal goes even further. The coil-sprung utility has a purposeful, workmanlike shape which makes no concessions to modern aerodynamic design. There's no mistaking a Defender, because it looks like no other vehicle, save the generations of 'working' Land Rovers whose distinctive outline has skipped easily from one decade to the next, from one series to the following one.

Defenders have always sat happily among the other products of Land Rover, sharing a technological philosophy with the Discovery and Range Rover which is unique to Soilhull. In the simplest, most basic analysis, only the bodies are different.

In writing this book I have not attempted to provide the detail of every last nut and bolt, each minute change, which took Land Rover from the first Series I to the birth of the One Ten in 1983, and from there to the introduction of the electronically sophisticated Td5. This has already been done so well and so thoroughly by others, in particular my good friend and colleague James Taylor.

Rather, I have set out to add to the enjoyment shared by so many of the entire Defender family, from inception to the present-day, with a book which is a mixture of celebration, information and confirmation. Celebration of the vehicles themselves, information to assist with purchase and ownership, and confirmation that the Defender is, indeed, all those things it is said to be.

Of course, it would have been wrong to produce a book on the Defender without looking back at the beginnings of the breed, and then charting the family's development through the years. The One Ten was an all-new vehicle when it was introduced, yet it took advantage of every lesson along the way, both from all the preceding Land Rovers and the Range Rover. You cannot write in depth about the Defender, already with a lifespan of 17 years, without looking also at those earlier machines.

In tracing the preceding vehicles I have deliberately focused on the highlights, those aspects which have had the most bearing on each succeeding model in turn, through to the One Ten and Ninety, and from there the Tdi-powered Defenders and on to the 21st century five-cylinder vehicles.

I have attempted to present information which is genuinely helpful. For example, the section dealing with the build up from prototype to launch of the first coil-sprung utility models helps to understand the present vehicle, while the detailed rundown of all nine engine types employed in the Defender family tells in detail what to expect from each, and hopefully will assist buyers in avoiding engines not suitable to their use of the vehicle.

The development of the enthusiast movement is explained, because without this there would be no need for a book of this kind, while the chapters dealing with ownership and preparation for off-roading reflect the progression from owner to enthusiast which is the inevitable consequence of buying a Land Rover.

The unrivalled capability of the Defender series optimises the enjoyment of off-roading activities, whether you're having an easy run on a green lane, or indulging in the more serious side of the pastime. (Nick Dimbleby)

This book is about the coil-sprung utilities, yet they cannot be viewed in isolation. Land Rover enthusiasm covers everything ... as I know so well from my own experience. I have owned various Land Rovers over the years, including leaf-sprung Series models, a 1983 One Ten V8 and several Range Rovers, and I now have a 200 Tdi Discovery. Defenders are the types I admire the most, yet I love the Discovery; however, my *favourite* Land Rover is the Series III Lightweight, a passion shared by Simon, my eldest son, who has an immaculate 1980 model of which I am extremely envious.

So, for Simon and all other Land Rover enthusiasts, I hope very much you will enjoy this book, even if you don't drive a Defender. And for those who are not quite so steeped in the magic elixir of Solihull I would like to think the following pages will be interesting and helpful.

Chapter **One**

From worker to cult machine

Not everybody finds it easy to understand why Land Rovers should excite enthusiasm. Discoverys and Range Rovers, certainly, but surely all other products of the world's most revered off-road manufacturer are noisy, uncomfortable, slow, thirsty and old-fashioned?

Well, yes, many of them are … up to a point.

But there's another side to the coin. Discoverys, Range Rovers, and Freelanders apart, all Land Rovers have about them an air of no-nonsense, down-to-earth, tough simplicity. They are honest about what they are, not knowing the meaning of pretentiousness; and although they were never intended to project an image of any kind, they make, in fact, the kind of lifestyle statement that other motor manufacturers would kill for. These days, this is what *sells* motor cars.

Whether it is the compact 90 or the spacious 110, the County Station Wagon is the most civilised version of the Defender, proving that Land Rovers do not have to be uncomfortable. (Nick Dimbleby)

It's fascinating to observe how Land Rovers were making these statements long before the concept of a 'lifestyle image' even existed. In the 1940s, '50s and '60s they were working machines which looked the part, with purposeful, clean-cut lines shouting toughness, versatility, and ability at everyone who saw them. They were among the first post-war vehicles to have a clearly identifiable image: there was no mistaking a Land Rover, either as a vehicle or for the things of which it was capable. If you drove one, you were associated with the hard realities of life in the remote out-doors; today, we call it lifestyle.

Then, in 1970, the Range Rover was thrust into the world, with a sleek, classic shape which was, at the same time, very evidently from the same gene pool as its working brothers. Since then, all utility Land Rovers have continued with the original family appearance which began in 1947 with the Series I, while all the luxury vehicles which have followed the original Range Rover have been carved in that vehicle's image. Thus two distinct family lines have been perpetuated. Yet crossing over between the two and linking them together is the familiarity of form you get between close cousins.

This master-stroke of family likeness which has been achieved at Solihull does not, in itself, explain why there's an enthusiast movement for Land Rovers without equal in any other single marque. But when you remember the other qualities of toughness and capability, and mix them into the pot with the looks and reputation, you begin to find the reasons why there's such a worldwide passion for anything and everything to have emerged from the factory at Lode Lane on Birmingham's south-eastern extremity.

First enthusiasts

That there would be an enthusiast movement centred on Land Rovers was inevitable from the day it was decided to put them into production. The first seeds of this passion were sown by the Willys Jeep, bought in large numbers when surplus wartime vehicles began to go on sale in 1945–6, primarily as working machines. Naturally, among the new owners were people who, despite petrol shortages, enjoyed the fun that Jeeps brought to motoring and who loved the thought of driving where other vehicles could not venture.

Then along came the Land Rover. Because it was a little more square cut, it had a more purposeful look about it than the Jeep which had inspired it, and was undeniably just as useful – if not a touch more so – when taken off the tarmac. Moreover it was British, from one of the world's most respected motor manufacturers.

The Land Rover was an incredibly appealing vehicle, and not all of this attraction could be explained in a logical manner. It was introduced as a working vehicle, for agriculture, forestry, and industry, but the interest in it went far beyond those definitions, and it wasn't long before motoring journalists were thinking, and writing, beyond the confines of the vehicle's advertised role.

In July 1948 the weekly magazine *Motor*

published, in two instalments, an extremely entertaining account of an expedition on some of the ancient routes in Mid-Wales in a Land Rover. This was the first off-roading story to be written involving a Land Rover and, given *Motor*'s great influence at the time, will have played a not inconsiderable part in extending the horizons of a vehicle which went into production that very month.

It was with the publication of these two articles that Land Rover's unique enthusiast movement was born, although nobody could have realised it at the time. Those first published words about the joys of off-roading in a Land Rover presaged something which over the next half-century and beyond would involve hundreds of thousands of people around the world, building with their enthusiasm a self-contained industry serving their needs, and ensuring the preservation of older models.

In June 1948, *Motor*'s E. H. Row and Joseph Lowrey, plus a photographer identified simply as Ross, drove their borrowed Land Rover from the factory and headed westward out of Birmingham. In complete contrast to today's well-equipped off-road enthusiasts, their only recovery aids for this first Land Rover leisure foray into a part of Wales seen as demanding even now, were a length of rope and, as it was described, 'a driving pulley for the power take-off for bollarding the car out if we did get stuck'.

Well, they did get stuck, and on one occasion had to recruit the assistance of 'five burly Welsh farmers' to help them out of a bog by hauling on the tow rope because there was nowhere to secure the rope for their 'bollarding'. They took the Land Rover down a track, never before driven in a motor vehicle, not even the Jeep owned by one of the

In all its forms the Defender family has always displayed the unmistakeable general outline that has lived for more than half a century in the 'working' Land Rovers. (Nick Dimbleby)

The original Land Rover, with its 80-inch wheelbase and stark simplicity, soon became a familiar sight on Britain's roads, and remains an extremely appealing vehicle. (Nick Dimbleby)

helpful farmers, with one of the party walking ahead to mark the edge, from which there was a precipitous drop. At the bottom they crossed the Towy river, thought hitherto not to be possible, then had to retrace their route because even the Land Rover could not get through the trees on the far side of the valley.

On the second day they made several ascents of Dunlop's Dividend, a particularly steep, hairpin-strewn climb near the village of Brechfa. The last climb was made with nine people somehow crammed in and on the Land Rover, five of them farmers. Indeed, *Motor*'s expedition must have served as a superb promotional event for the Rover Motor Company, because the reports commented on the great interest shown in the vehicle by farmers at every stop.

More importantly – because farmers would in due course buy Land Rovers anyway, especially as times became gradually less harsh – the two articles in this opinion-forming motoring magazine told the world that the Land Rover was a car people could enjoy. There were already motorists

who enjoyed cross-country driving for fun, doing surprisingly well in cars as ordinary as Austin Sevens, and this first account of an off-roading journey in a Land Rover was a significant milestone for the recently-launched four-wheel drive from Solihull.

By 1955 the Series I had become fully established as a working vehicle and, perhaps to the surprise of many at Rover, was already a part of the motoring scene, having developed a passionate following with people who wanted the extra capability and character that ordinary cars just could not bring them.

Probably the first major expedition undertaken by a privately owned Land Rover finished in London in the summer of that year. Just as the off-roading trip to Mid-Wales was to establish the Land Rover as the ideal vehicle for mountain track driving, this year-long trek showed the world that when it came to extended overlanding the Land Rover was the vehicle to use.

Started just six years after the Land Rover was introduced, this trailblazing journey was the most extensive trip, other than circumnavigation, that it is possible to make – all the way from Australia to Britain. It began on the island of Tasmania, off Australia's south-eastern coast, and for good measure began with a sightseeing tour around most of Australia, before sailing to Ceylon. From there, the route wound through India, then directly west through the Middle East, from Istanbul into Europe, and finally across the Channel back to Britain.

The three people – two men and a woman – who made this journey had fitted the Land Rover 80-inch with a special body providing sleeping space, and towed a trailer which had been specially constructed so that it could be fitted on to the Land Rover's bonnet for sea crossings, thereby avoiding extra shipping costs.

The adventure was fully reported in *Motor* in August 1955. The entire journey, even more arduous then than now because of the lack of metalled roads, was undertaken without serious mechanical difficulties, punctures being the chief problem. As is the case with Land Rover expeditions today, the vehicle was pressed into use on several occasions to rescue the stranded vehicles of other travellers.

There's nothing more demanding than an overland trip from Australia to Britain, especially when it begins with a grand tour Down Under, and the fact that three people did just this in an 80-inch Land Rover in 1954–5 added fuel to the fire as far as the enthusiast movement was concerned.

The One Ten's first adventure

An off-roading adventure with a One Ten in the Western Highlands of Scotland was reported in

David Mitchell runs the world's largest Land Rover model shop from his offices in Bala, North Wales, and somehow finds time to organise a wide variety of off-road training activites, as well as officiating at major off-road events. He is seen here with two of his vehicles, a Defender 110 and a Range Rover. (Dave Barker)

detail in a motoring magazine in the same week as the new Land Rover was introduced at the Geneva Motor Show in March 1983.

The Trident Green V8 County Station Wagon CWK 20Y was driven by *Autocar* a couple of weeks before the launch in a bid to find out just how good the new vehicle was. The journey included 85mph (137kph) motorway cruising and, after the short ferry crossing to Skye, some driving on one of the island's tracks – during which the journalists got themselves stuck, requiring rescue.

Later, they drove part of General Wade's Military Road, an epic cross-country route, which the team entered near Fort Augustus at the southern end of Loch Ness. On reaching impossibly deep snow they decided to turn round, only to get one wheel stuck in a very deep pothole with the chassis sitting on ice. The only way out was to jack up each corner in turn, using the standard wheel-change jack, and build up the surface beneath the wheels.

Despite the problems which, they failed to admit, were mostly of their own making, they rated the new vehicle very highly. It was, in fact, a far-sighted story to publish; even before the One Ten was officially launched, it had been apparent to *Autocar* that this was just the sort of use people would be putting it to in the years to come.

It was a good and prophetic first for the magazine.

Model mania

The press was universally enthusiastic about the Land Rover, which undoubtedly encouraged the feeling of warmth many motorists also felt towards it. In 1955 the *Woodworker* magazine showed in great detail how to make an extremely realistic wooden model.

Model making was an important component of the hobby scene in the days before television ruled our lives, and the *Woodworker* Land Rover model would not have been devised and published had the editor not felt there was an enthusiastic following for the vehicle. The model, constructed in plywood and hardboard, was exceptionally realistic. The overall length wasn't given, but the sides were 1ft 2in (0.36m) long, making it quite large.

DID YOU KNOW?

One Ten 6x6
Within months of introducing the One Ten, Land Rover had produced a prototype six-wheel-drive version. It was finished in sand colour, sported XS sand tyres, and had a number of military fitments – so no guesses regarding who it was aimed at. The prototype was fitted with a V8 engine driving the front axle and forward rear axle permanently, as standard. Drive to the third axle was engaged via a dog clutch in the second axle, operated when the centre diff lock was engaged, and sharing the centre diff lock's vacuum. While the standard One Ten was fitted with a Salisbury rear axle, the 6x6 used standard Land Rover axles throughout.

Since those days, interest in model Land Rovers has kept pace with the enthusiast movement generally, reflecting popular passion for the vehicle. By the time the One Ten appeared in 1983 Land Rover models had been well established in their own right for several decades, and self-build modelling remains very much part of the Land Rover world. However, today's do-it-yourself enthusiasts use kits with parts prefabricated in plastic and white metal. The detail can be impressive: recent introductions include 1/76 scale models of the British Army's Defender XD Wolf, with such options as Fitted-for-Radio or non FFR, right- or left-hand drive, and alternative 'handed' windscreen wipers.

That the model scene mirrors the general enthusiasm for Land Rovers, and in some ways provides a barometer of enthusiasm for the real thing, is evidenced by the mini-industry which has developed around it. Commercial leader of the Land Rover model world is David Mitchell, who runs the world's largest dedicated-marque model business in parallel with his Landcraft off-road training centre at Bala in North Wales. Dave has a stock list of more than 500 items – all of them Land Rovers – and sells to customers around the

From early days the Series I has been a favourite machine for trials competitors, where agility and excellent ground clearance are important. (Nick Dimbleby)

world. The business developed from his own interest in miniature Land Rovers which, in turn, had grown out of a life-long involvement with the vehicles. The earliest Land Rover model of which Dave is aware is a Dinky version of a Mersey Tunnel Police Series I 80-inch, produced when the 80-inch was in production. There may be even older ones.

The Series I has always been the most popular model within the range, followed by the Lightweight, and remains so despite a growing passion for models of the Defender range – itself the most popular type of Land Rover with today's enthusiasts.

Competition

The dual facts that the Association of Rover Clubs (ARC) celebrated its 50th birthday in 1998, and that its member clubs are almost exclusively for Land Rover enthusiasts, says a great deal about the longevity of the Land Rover enthusiast movement.

The Range Rover was a success from the start, stimulating further interest in Land Rovers generally, as well as exceeding expectations in its own right. The original body lines, as in this very early example, were destined to remain fundamentally unchanged until the first series went out of production a quarter of a century later. (Nick Dimbleby)

True, at one time there were far more saloon car owners represented beneath the ARC's umbrella, but it is inescapable that the association would have long since disappeared but for the passion of Land Rover owners.

Competition has always played an important role for such enthusiasts. Indeed, it was the use of Land Rovers in off-road trials from about 1950 onwards which sparked the first truly active beginnings of the enthusiast movement. These car trials, like their two-wheel counterparts, are practically as old as motor vehicles, but they became especially popular in the years between the First and Second World Wars.

This passion for pitting machine and driver against terrain chosen for its difficulty was quick to return after the war, adding a sense of excitement to the dreariness of the late 1940s. Within a few months of the first Land Rovers coming into general ownership in the second half of 1948, it was apparent that in any form of competition involving off-road hill climbs and mud, the Land Rover was, quite literally, in a class of its own. It didn't take long for special competitions for the four-wheel drive vehicles to come into being. Remember, except for the Jeep there were no other 4x4s available, and by now a great many Jeeps had fallen by the wayside because of the lack of spare parts.

The original Land Rover, despite its lack of power, was a brilliant trials car. The degree of traction was astonishing to people more accustomed to Austin 7 specials and the like, while the high ground clearance and tiny, 80-inch

wheelbase gave it a niftiness through tightly marked sections, often over tree roots and rocks, which competitors loved.

Land Rovers developed, first to the 86-inch and then 88-inch Series Is, then Series IIs, IIAs and IIIs, and then into the ultimate incarnation of the breed, the Ninety. But, throughout, the original 80-inch remained the favourite of triallers, although many different, and always more powerful, engines were experimented with.

The ultimate trials car, however, was not destined to arrive until someone had the inspiration to fit a Rover V8 engine into a Series I 80-inch chassis. It is not known when this was done for the first time, although it was certainly

Well before the launch of the first of the Defender family, greenlaning had been a popular form of off-roading for owners of leaf-sprung Land Rovers. Comfort levels were not up to those of the later coil-sprung vehicles, though. (Nick Dimbleby)

before the launch of the Range Rover in 1970.

Passion for the V8 as a trials engine intensified when people realised just how supreme the Range Rover was in off-road situations. In turn, the Range Rover made life easier for trials enthusiasts, for much-modified versions of that vehicle's permanent four-wheel drive transmission were transplanted into many a trialler, overcoming the hitherto almost insurmountable problem of finding a transmission that was tough enough to survive the torque of the V8 in competition, yet was suitable for four-wheel drive.

For many years it was this passion for the Series I and, of course, other Land Rovers as competitive machinery which drove the enthusiast movement. The machines' capabilities drew trials enthusiasts to them, while the spin-off was a growing general interest in Land Rovers for off-road enjoyment.

Then, in the 1960s, the interest in recreational vehicles began to develop in its own right as

The Discovery is enormously popular with enthusiasts, who admire its unique mixture of comfort, space, off-roading ability and value-for-money. Here, the off-road stability is being put to the test. (Nick Dimbleby)

owners started to look upon the motor car as more than the functional machine it had been in the decade or so following the end of hostilities in 1945. To begin with the Land Rover had it all its own way, and a great many Series IIs and IIAs were bought by people eager to extend their leisure time with camping, caravanning, and boating, for which the Land Rover was perfect, but by the time the Range Rover appeared on the scene there was also considerable 4x4 choice from the USA and Japan.

However, the Range Rover refocused attention on Solihull machinery, and the growing movement was given a big shot in the arm by wild enthusiasm for the new vehicle. You had to be pretty well-off to afford one – in its first year the Range Rover cost

£2,000 (compared with £1,300 for an MGB GT) – but the rave reviews stimulated many less well-off buyers into choosing Series III Station Wagons instead.

By 1980 Land Rover devotees were among the most passionate of all motorists. However, it was the Defender family which would have the most positive impact on Land Rover enthusiasm. I remember very clearly returning from the 1983 Geneva Motor Show, launch pad of the One Ten, positively burning with praise for what Land Rover had achieved. This, in turn, spurred me to persuade my employers, IPC, to allow me to launch Britain's first full-scale, glossy, 4x4 magazine, *4-Wheel Drive*, to compete with David Bowyer's *Overlander* newsletter, itself about to be turned into the glossy publication *Off-Road*. My own launch, in 1984, coincided more or less with the introduction of the Ninety.

The mid-1980s were a great turning point for the Land Rover movement, which was already a force to be reckoned with. Though the two new magazines were not dedicated solely to Land Rovers the Solihull marque inevitably dominated both. And in enthusiast terms the Ninety has shown itself to be the most significant vehicle produced by Land Rover. A number of specialist companies dedicated to supplying parts for older models also made their first appearance at this time, and some of them, such as John Craddock, have since grown into world-renowned organisations.

The two specialist magazines were a natural marketplace for four-wheel drive enthusiasts and the traders who relied on them, and served to stimulate further the growing interest in off-road driving for fun, and recreational 4x4 vehicles.

But other events also encouraged growing interest in four-wheel drive. By 1985 the 4x4

This is the first prototype of the Ninety, with a 90-inch wheelbase, and now lives alongside the second prototype, which had the production wheelbase of 92.9in, at the Dunsfold Collection in Surrey. (James Taylor)

products of Japanese manufacturers were being promoted heavily and were selling well, considerably raising the profile of off-road vehicles. This process in turn would, in due course, be good for the Land Rover movement. Most of the Far Eastern vehicles were good products, with high standards of comfort, light controls, good looks, and excellent engines and gearboxes.

Yet, for all the appeal of Japanese 4x4s – the Mitsubishi Shogun, in particular, being quite capable of out-performing Land Rovers (but not the Range Rover) in all respects other than difficult off-roading – enthusiasm for Land Rovers remained unaffected. Many users of working Land Rovers, farmers in particular, switched to Mitsubishi, Daihatsu, and Isuzu at about this time, as did plenty of people in the Range Rover marketplace, but within a few years they would

Defenders, and Defender-based 'specials' are extremely useful vehicles for safari companies in Southern Africa, and have introduced many a previously indifferent motorist to the advantages of Land Rovers. (Nick Dimbleby)

mostly have returned to Solihull machinery.

All this time club membership was growing quite rapidly. Competition, which had done so much to establish the Land Rover enthusiast movement, began to take second place to fun off-roading, with a steady influx of Land Rovers on to Britain's network of green lanes, and the establishment of purpose-designed off-road driving centres. The first off-road driving schools began to do quite well.

Then, in 1987, the world's first specialist Land Rover magazine appeared in the form of *Land Rover Owner*. The new publication was both a measure of how far the enthusiast movement had come, and the catalyst for much of the rapid growth thereafter.

The magazine came at just the right time. The One Ten and Ninety had been around for four and three years respectively, and were popular with enthusiasts, many of whom used the new vehicles to replace their old Series IIIs. In other cases the sheer attractiveness and capability of the coil-sprung Land Rovers brought fresh faces into the fold.

From this point on the Land Rover's dedicated followers grew rapidly in numbers, the movement getting a further shot in the arm with the running of the first Land Rover show at Billing Aquadrome, Northampton, in 1990. Organised by the original management team of *Land Rover Owner*, headed by the dynamic Richard Green, this annual event has ever since brought together countless thousands of enthusiasts in the celebration of all things Land Rover. The show, and the magazine with which it was associated, played a major role in cementing the various factions of the movement into a cohesive whole, particularly in its first five years.

'Billing', as it is known by Land Rover people worldwide, is by far the largest and most important event of its type. As a single-marque jamboree it has no equal.

Into the future

It is an inescapable fact that the Defender series of vehicles has been particularly significant in the development of the Land Rover movement. There's the obvious appeal to the keen off-roader, of

course, but the sheer usefulness of the range, and the family-carrying ability of the One Ten in particular, makes them especially suitable for anybody who enjoys the outdoor life. Many a camping or caravanning family has bought a Defender 110 purely because of its appeal as a lifestyle-related vehicle, and has then found within weeks that they've become enthusiasts.

The Discovery, too, has been important, with many owners finding unexpected enthusiasm after years of driving large, but extremely bland, estate cars and other 4x4s. Existing enthusiasts, too, have taken to this vehicle, in some cases adding, say, a five-year-old Discovery to, perhaps, a Series Land Rover. The Billing Show, always a barometer of ownership, has seen a marked increase in enthusiast-owned Discoverys over recent years.

And, as ever, the Range Rover remains highly popular. Attend any gathering of Land Rover people and there will always be an assortment of Range Rovers – maybe ancient, and obviously well past their best, sometimes alongside nearly new 'mark IIs'.

That the enthusiast movement has been important to the sales of more modern Land Rovers is beyond doubt. Land Rover itself, at one time slow to even acknowledge the existence of enthusiasts, now makes much of its heritage and is eager to participate at major events.

There seems little doubt that the movement will continue to flourish, and that the Defender will remain central to it. With greater emphasis than ever before on environmental issues, it is possible that some off-roading activities may come under pressure, but this is unlikely to harm the movement in any way.

It is thought that the massive success of the Freelander, which seems set to introduce more people to Land Rover ownership than any other model, will be generally good for both club memberships and general enthusiasm, as owners seek to explore the more-extensive capabilities of the Defender – the ultimate Land Rover.

In some ways, the enormously appealing Defender is safeguarding the future of the movement. It will surely continue in this role for many years to come.

Legends are made of this

The birth of Land Rover is one of the most oft-repeated stories in the history of motoring. It's a tale of inspiration and determination, of great timing and imaginative engineering and, above all, it's a story about making the most out of difficult circumstances. Yet for all that, the story of the subsequent success of first the machine, and then the Land Rover marque, is perhaps even more remarkable.

The original Land Rover was thrown together extremely rapidly, based to no small degree on the Second World War's ubiquitous Jeep. Using whatever components happened to be available within the Rover organisation, in a factory in which production was otherwise virtually at a standstill,

The machine which started the legend was simply called a Land Rover, and only became known as Series I when the second series was introduced in April 1958. Originally, it was seen merely as a stop-gap vehicle, providing production in an otherwise little-used factory amid the austerity of post-war Britain. (Nick Dimbleby)

the Land Rover was intended as no more than a stop-gap earner to tide the company over until real money began pouring into its coffers when the post-war world woke up to the enormous attractions of Rover cars. But, as is often the way, subsequent events failed to stick to the script.

Demand for the Land Rover exceeded all expectations by a very long way, while there were very few buyers for Rover's cars, which were little more than reawakened pre-war models. The Land Rover became better, but the cars failed to pull themselves out of the high-quality, yet stuffy mould which, before the war, had served the company well. The Land Rover production lines became ever more important to Rover's precarious finances, and the short-term lifespan intended for the utility machine evolved into permanence.

The Jeep's influence

The true beginning of the Land Rover story does not go back to the advent of four-wheel drive technology in the earliest days of the 20th century, nor to the all-terrain tanks of the First World War,

but to the best-known and best-loved vehicle of the Second World War: the Jeep.

The wartime Jeep was to have a profound and permanent influence because it inspired the development of four-wheel-drive motoring throughout much of the world. Most importantly, in the post-war period the Jeep's qualities were to lead to the Land Rover. For that reason alone the Jeep's story is one which should not be forgotten or overlooked.

Entering service in 1941, the Jeep was the result of a far-sighted decision by the US military that, because it seemed inevitable that America would be drawn into the war raging in Europe, there would be enormous advantages in having a lightweight, general purpose, four-wheel-drive vehicle. As everybody knows, the resultant vehicle became known as the 'Jeep' because of its 'General

This is the machine which played an important part in the Second World War, the Willys Jeep, and which inspired the creation of the Land Rover during 1947. (James Taylor Collection)

Purpose' (GP) classification. Prototypes were built with astonishing speed, in order to meet the urgency dictated in its specification requirement of June 1940. Quickest to appear was that of the Bantam Car Company, closely followed by Willys-Overland, and Ford. In the event, Bantam was unable to meet production requirements, despite coming up with the best design, and Willys got the contract, although many of the Bantam's features were incorporated. Though Ford was beaten by Willys because the latter's engine was better, Ford nevertheless produced a quarter of a million Jeeps under licence, compared to the 360,000 built by Willys by the end of the war.

Wartime service wasn't the end of the Jeep story in America, with non-military versions proving popular amongst various user groups from 1945 onwards. In Britain, though, there was no prospect of buying a foreign-built vehicle at the time – or at least, not a new one.

Jeeps had been a very familiar sight on British roads throughout America's participation in the war, and people liked them. More to the point,

many British servicemen had seen them in action, and had been highly impressed. Many of the Jeeps which survived the war were sold off in Britain at the end of hostilities, and such was the vehicle's reputation and usefulness – especially to farmers, whose only means of cross-country transport hitherto had been by tractor or horse – that any Jeep in working order was sure to find a buyer.

One was snapped up by Maurice Wilks, not just a farmer but also Rover's Chief Engineer, who found the little truck perfect in the mud of his rain-soaked Welsh farm. The story goes that Maurice's brother Spencer asked what he would do when the Jeep wore out, spares not being available, and Maurice promptly stated he would buy another Jeep. 'Why don't we build our own?' one is alleged to have said to the other.

Originally it was thought that a centre-steer design would simplify production because it would be suitable for left and right-hand drive markets. However, the prototype showed it was not such a good idea, and the concept was dropped. (James Taylor Collection)

It might be much more capable, more comfortable and a lot bigger, but the Defender Td5 which took Land Rover into the 21st century is related directly to the first of the line. (Nick Dimbleby)

One problem, and there were many, was that Rover's Board still saw its future in cars, and they didn't want to commit themselves to anything which might get in the way of car production once they had a new medium-sized saloon ready. But the huge Solihull factory – German bombers had destroyed the company's principal factory and head offices in Coventry in 1940 – could not sit idle. It had to start producing something, and was obliged to play a role in the all-important export drive, one of the few ways of bringing desperately needed foreign money into Britain.

Following the conversation between Maurice and Spencer Wilks, Rover's Gordon Bashford went off to buy a couple of surplus Jeeps ... and the Land Rover story began. Maurice Wilks reputedly came up with the new vehicle's name during that same fortuitous conversation.

Rapid popularity

Given the extremely enthusiastic following the Jeep had built up in its own short but important lifetime, it is not at all surprising that the Land Rover would quickly achieve enormous popularity, which in turn developed into a cult status similar to that enjoyed by the Willys Jeep.

Under the direction of Robert Boyle – but with Maurice Wilks keeping a fatherly eye on everything – the design of the Land Rover began to take shape in the second quarter of 1947. It was a stop-gap vehicle, remember, so expensive tooling was not part of the plan, and this dictated the welded steel chassis and, for production vehicles, simply formed body panels with a marked absence of curves. Steel was a rare commodity and supplies were mainly restricted to guaranteed export business, so only the chassis and mechanical parts would be steel; on the other hand, there was plenty of aluminium which, although much more expensive than steel, had the extra advantage of being easier to work by hand.

In order to make it possible to utilise a single production line for both home and export orders it was felt that a centre-steer vehicle would be ideal, so this was the format of the first prototype completed in mid-1947. The Jeep influence at this stage was quite profound, with an open, door-less body, curved wings and wheel arches, and even a Jeep chassis – although this was because Rover's own design wasn't yet complete.

By the time the first pilot build vehicles were emerging from Solihull, very early in 1948, things had changed considerably. Gone were centre steering, curved wings, and some of the wheel arch sweep, along with the feeble 1,389cc engine of the prototypes, which had been used in the pre-war Rover 10. It was these pilot build Land Rovers which were used to launch the vehicle at the Amsterdam Motor Show in April 1948, and to demonstrate the usefulness of Rover's new utility machine at agricultural shows around Britain during the following few months. Full production

DID YOU KNOW?

Speed limit

The fact that the first Land Rovers could hardly exceed 50mph (80kph) was not at all a problem for drivers of the day, and the performance of the vehicles should be viewed in this context.

The Land Rover had been classified by the authorities as a commercial vehicle, although to be truthful there had been considerable uncertainty as to its proper place in law. In the post-war period all commercial vehicles were limited to a maximum speed of 30mph (48kph), and woe betide the driver of any commercial who went faster. Consequently, Land Rovers trundled along at the same speed as coal delivery lorries and the like. However, by the 1950s people were beginning to question the 30mph limit for light commercial vehicles and, although it was very rare to see any car – other than the occasional Jaguar – doing more than about 55mph (88kph) Land Rover drivers in particular were starting to feel aggrieved.

An appeal to the Law Lords in 1956 against a speeding conviction settled the matter, and Land Rovers were decreed to be car-type vehicles, thus freeing them from the 30mph restriction.

commenced in July 1948, an amazing achievement for traditionally slow-moving Rover.

As far as most customers were concerned, the first production vehicles were the same as the ones they'd seen in demonstrations. They were pick-ups, finished in light green, but significant differences included re-routeing the exhaust to the right-hand side instead of the left, non-galvanised chassis, and bolt-on front bumper. Power came from a slightly modified version of the 1,595cc inlet-over-exhaust engine developed for the P3 saloon, as was the gearbox, with the useful addition of a step-down ratio and permanent four-wheel drive with a freewheel system in the front driveline.

Nobody knew it, but this was the forerunner of the entire family, the patriarch which would establish the Land Rover as the principal go-anywhere working vehicle throughout much of the world. Its immediate success, and the passions it aroused, surprised most of those who had been connected with its development, not least Rover's Board of Directors.

Prophetically, Rover's Chairman announced a few days before Christmas 1948 – a time when good news was hard to come by in austerity-stricken post-war Britain – that the level of orders already received pointed to the possibility of Land Rover output exceeding the company's car production figures. A year later it had done just that.

Direct line

Today's Defender is a direct descendant of the 1948 Land Rover, and it's a great tribute to the original design that you could place a Land Rover built in 2000 in a time machine, take it back to 1948, and see it recognised instantly. The appearance of the original machine might have been a product of necessity and austerity, but it's a shape which has stood the test of time better than that of any other motor vehicle.

Although quite a snug fit, there was ample working space around the 1.6-litre engine in the early Series I 80-inch models. (James Taylor Collection)

Land Rover tried very hard to project the Series I as a vehicle suitable for hard work on the farm. This photograph shows a 107-inch earning its keep. (James Taylor Collection)

The square-cut lines of a Land Rover denote a functionality which is unique, and which in the Land Rover is very much more than skin deep. Today's Land Rover is altogether more competent than the vehicle which started it all – and so it should be after more than five decades of steady development – but the 1948 Land Rover was just as capable of doing everything asked of it as today's Td5.

Nobody really knows for sure, but it is quite probable that when Maurice Wilks appointed Robert Boyle to head up the small project team which gave the world the Land Rover, he thought no further than giving farmers like himself a vehicle which would make life easier. It was only as the project began to take shape that the export potential began to dawn – hence the attempt, initially, to produce it with central steering – and it was only after the Amsterdam Motor Show launch that the vehicle's appeal to other user groups, including private individuals, started to show through.

It's tempting, today, to relate everything to the way things are done now, with car makers producing vehicles aimed at clearly identified, and verified, market sectors. That a single individual had the idea for a vehicle, and that the vehicle itself then attracted the user groups to it, seems remarkable. But that's the way things were when the Land Rover came into being.

Again, seen from today's perspective the original Land Rover might seem a pretty uninspiring

DID YOU KNOW?

Production milestones

There's only one true measure of success in the tough world of automotive manufacturing, and that's how well any particular vehicle sells. Given the highly specialist nature of the earliest Land Rovers, and the very slow start in 1948, it is quite astonishing that production had risen to around 18,000 vehicles a year by 1950, and that it took only six years to hit the 100,000 mark. In those days figures like this were respectable by any standard. By comparison, Rover's total saloon car production between 1948 and 1954, with its P3 and first P4 models, was 53,000 units. Land Rover landmarks were:

1954	100,000
1959	250,000
1966	500,000
1971	750,000
1976	1,000,000

vehicle. The inlet-over-exhaust 1,595cc engine gave it a top speed of around 50mph (80kph), with 40-45mph (65–72kph) cruising, and it was extremely basic: you paid extra for doors, side-screens, canvas roof for the cab, passenger seat, and starting handle. But the price until October 1948 was only £450, and even the huge jump from this to £540 including the extras, left the vehicle within the 'affordable' category for most potential users. There's also the point that, at the time, even many everyday cars could not pass 60mph (96kph) and were seriously lacking in creature comforts.

The simplicity and functionality appealed greatly to a small number of motoring journalists who were among the first non-Rover people to drive the Land Rover. On 30 April 1948 *Commercial Motor* wrote in glowing terms, under the headline 'A maid-of-all-work for the farmer', about the outstanding features of this new Rover. The magazine was enthusiastic about the sturdiness of the engine, and commended Rover for giving the vehicle such an excellent cooling system with the needs of stationary work in mind. In its detailed description of the transmission it commented on the wisdom of the freewheel device incorporated into the front drive from the transfer box. Rover was also praised for providing, uniquely, three auxiliary power points: at the front for a mechanical winch; the main power take-off provision at the rear; and the central power take-off facility for powering portable plant carried inside the vehicle.

Less concerned with the pure working nature of the Land Rover was *Autocar*, whose first description of the vehicle, also on 30 April 1948, contained a number of far-seeing comments. 'So much has been said and written in the past about the so-called People's Car, much of it nonsense, that the advent of a really practical British vehicle which goes far beyond that over-publicised proposal should be hailed with genuine acclamation', stated one of Britain's most-respected magazines. The article went on: 'If the world has to be strictly economical for years to come, is not this the sort of car that most of us need, one that is entirely practical and essentially usable?'

Comments like this led to considerable early interest in the Land Rover, which grew to fever pitch over the next few months as potential users were able to view the few demonstrators available and, if they were very lucky, to have a brief test drive. By the end of that year the future of the Land Rover was beginning to look very secure.

On the farm

The massive enthusiasm generated within a few months of the first Land Rovers becoming available illustrates vividly just how right the vehicle was, and how timely was its introduction. Yet it was in some ways less useful on the farm than Land Rover's advertising would have you believe.

The most outstanding of post-war agricultural innovations was the much-loved Ferguson tractor, produced in very large numbers by Standard from 1946, which gave farmers the working power they needed at the time. This could pull ploughs,

---

DID YOU KNOW?

Purchase tax

Levels of purchase tax varied in the austere years following the Second World War but were, to put it mildly, punitive. As late as 1959 (a year after the introduction of the Series II), the price differential between basic Land Rovers, which did not attract purchase tax, and Station Wagons, which did, was considerable:

Model	Basic body	Station Wagon
88-inch	£650	£1,049
109-inch	£730	£1,219

Most of the extra cost of the Station Wagons was purchase tax, a factor which inhibited sales and actually influenced manufacturing decisions. In the first year of Land Rover production, a very pretty Station Wagon was built on the 80-inch chassis and introduced at the Commercial Motor Show in October 1948. Despite having very pleasant lines, seating for seven, winding windows in the front doors and other refinements, purchase tax pushed the price so high that few customers were found, and the vehicle was discontinued in 1951.

harrows, rollers, and harvesting binders, and had power-take-off and pulley drive (for threshing machines, pumps, circular saws, etc). Rover attempted to portray the Land Rover as being capable of most of these same duties, but, in truth, it could not plough and wasn't much use for much of the other field work that tractors and horses took in their stride. Though by the early 1950s horses were beginning to fade out from heavy work, they were replaced by tractors, not Land Rovers.

However, since the owners of most smaller farms could not afford to run two cars (many couldn't afford even one), Land Rovers began to replace some of their existing vehicles – including wartime Jeeps as they wore out. This is how the Land Rover started to become a permanent feature of British rural life. Only on large farms, which in 1948–50 were few and far between, were Land Rovers bought to work alongside tractors.

In truth, it didn't take very long for Rover to realise that the new vehicle had limited appeal as an agricultural machine, although it was continually promoted as such, and orders came in from a much wider selection of buyers than had been expected. This encouraged Rover to introduce its Station Wagon at the 1948 Commercial Motor Show. This was a delightful seven-seater based on

This publicity photograph was taken for the launch of the Series II 109-inch, a wheelbase destined to become highly popular around the world, accounting for three-quarters of Land Rover sales. The 109-inch was introduced towards the end of Series I production, for the 1957 model year. (James Taylor Collection)

the standard 80-inch chassis, but it only lasted until 1951, principally because of its high price.

Important early developments were the dropping of the freewheel for the 1951 model year, replacing it with a dog clutch, and the facility of two-wheel drive in high gears as an alternative to the permanent four-wheel drive in low ratios. Another key move, during 1951, was the introduction of a 1,997cc engine, derived from the original 1.5-litre unit. But this engine was not used for long, and a new unit with the same dimensions was introduced in late 1953, overshadowed by the launch at the same time of the more useful 86-inch model (which replaced the 80-inch) and the all-new 107-inch vehicle, available initially only as a pick-up.

Pointing the way forward, a second seven-seat Station Wagon was introduced in 1954, based on the more practical 86-inch body. This was followed two years later by the very appealing ten-seat Station Wagon built on the 107-inch frame.

In late 1956 both wheelbase types gained an

extra two inches, the resulting 88-inch and 109-inch versions being destined to remain in service until they were replaced by the Ninety and One Ten vehicles, which later became the Defender. The reason for the extra length was the introduction, although not until June 1957, of Land Rover's first diesel engine, a 2,052cc unit specially developed by Rover for its 4x4.

So, with a choice of petrol and diesel engines, 88-inch and 109-inch chassis, and different body types, the legend of the Land Rover was firmly in the making. And this was before the end of the first series.

Birthday party

The tenth birthday of the Land Rover was celebrated in great style, and what better way to acknowledge the huge success of Rover's 'stop-gap', production-filling, post-war vehicle than with

the introduction of a second version?

The Series II, launched in April 1958, was 1.5in (38mm) wider and looked a little sleeker, with some slight curves to parts of the body to reduce the hard angularity of the Series I, more shaping to the bonnet panel, lower body sides hiding the exhaust pipe and chassis sides, and neater door hinges. There was no mistaking it for a Land Rover – indeed, you had to know your Land Rovers to be able to tell it was a different vehicle – and in making the new model so like the one it replaced Solihull's designers and engineers had laid the groundwork for one of the vehicle's more important characteristics for the physical similarity of the entire Land Rover family, from Series I to

One of the less well-known engines in the Land Rover story is the six-cylinder 2,652cc IOE unit introduced for the 1967 model year in the Series IIA 109-inch. (James Taylor Collection)

Defender, has proved an important factor in ongoing enthusiasm for the marque.

Of course, things had to change mechanically, and at Land Rover changes have very often been for the better, unlike many car companies. The key development introduced with the Series II was the use of the 2,286cc petrol engine, giving 25bhp more than the 2-litre unit it replaced and, as time would tell, immense reliability and ruggedness.

The new engine was, in fact, a development of the 2,052cc diesel unit. It was to prove a crucial power plant for Land Rover, and lived long enough to be used in the One Ten in 1983 and in Series IIIs produced for two years after that. Unfortunately, early buyers of 88-inch Series IIs had to make do with the old petrol engine until supplies had been used up, although the new engine was fitted in the 109-inch. And if you wanted a Station Wagon, you had to make do with the old-model 107-inch

because the 109-inch Series II Station Wagon was not ready until several months later.

The Series II was more than a re-engined and (slightly) restyled version of what had gone before. Its extra width made it more stable on side slopes and gave it a better steering lock. The ride, too, was better. The Series II gave way to the Series IIA in early Autumn 1961. A very significant introduction at the same time – but not the reason for the IIA designation, which was to permit a new chassis numbering system throughout Rover – was the upgrading of the diesel to 2,286cc, giving it

The Range Rover, with its long-travel springs and extreme axle articulation, set new standards of off-road performance from its first days, as this shot of the amazing vehicle displays. It was to be 13 years after the Range Rover's launch before this sort of performance would be possible with a utility model.
(Nick Dimbleby)

more power and torque and much better reliability.

Other than the introduction of the Forward Control version on the 109-inch chassis, little of importance happened to the 88-inch and 109-inch utilities, other than the introduction of the 2,652cc six-cylinder engine option for the long wheelbase in 1967. This engine remained an option in the subsequent Series III until the Stage 1 V8 was introduced in 1980.

Range Rover's influence

The Range Rover was launched in June 1970 and was destined to have a profound effect on the fortunes of Land Rover as well as a major impact on the leisure four-wheel drive market. Last, but not least, it would greatly influence the technical thinking of the fourth generation of 'working' Land Rovers in 13 years' time.

Although Solihull's production lines had been turning out Land Rovers for 22 years, the Range Rover was the company's first genuinely new vehicle since the Series I. It would revolutionise 4x4

thinking so much that by the time production of what was then known as the Classic finally ceased in 1996 it was still the undisputed class leader.

It came on to the market a full year before the Series IIA Land Rover gave way to the Series III, yet not one aspect of the Range Rover's advanced technical specification was used in the Series III – although, if Solihull had wished to take the plunge, it could have continued the Series IIA for another couple of years, and then brought out a mechanically advanced Series III. This was not to be, however, and it was left entirely to the Range Rover to establish the principles of low-rate long-travel coil springs, extreme axle articulation, permanent four-wheel drive, and high standards of performance and comfort.

Land Rover's reluctance to apply the benefits of

Although introduced after the Range Rover, the Series III Land Rover remained a very basic machine. The concessions to more car-like qualities included an improved dash and all-synchro gearbox. (Nick Dimbleby)

the Range Rover to the utility range can be explained by the conservatism of the markets the latter served, and by a shortage of cash. Both are good reasons, but the fact remains that Solihull had, in the Range Rover, the basis for entirely fresh thinking in its range of 'working' models. Nobody will ever know how much harm was done by not moving faster.

Growing enthusiasm

By the time the Series III was introduced in September 1971 there was already, as we have seen, an enthusiast movement. Furthermore, the launch of the Range Rover in 1970 had resulted in a great deal of marque awareness among groups not in the 'front line' of Solihull's customers.

Only the reasonably well-off could afford a Range Rover, but people were now looking towards Land Rover for everyday and leisure vehicles. The Series IIA had been quite difficult for some people to drive, with its absence of synchromesh on the lower two gears, but there were no such problems

with the all-synchro Series III. The dash, too, was more car-like, and although all versions were now fitted with a 9.5-inch heavy-duty clutch, the pedal operating pressure was reduced considerably.

At the time the Series III arrived in the showrooms Land Rover had manufactured nearly 800,000 vehicles. Some 75 per cent of annual production was being exported, and although many of the overseas markets were still more than happy with the simple nature of the Land Rover, the situation was destined to change, both at home and abroad, as the end of the 1970s approached.

At the beginning of the decade there was little opposition to the Land Rover, either as a working or a leisure vehicle, but as the 1980s loomed, on the horizon there were genuine alternatives, and Japan was getting in on the 4x4 act. Those people

The first factory-produced Land Rover with good road-going performance was the Stage 1 V8, available only in the 109-inch version, and retaining the leaf springing of the rest of the Series III models. (Nick Dimbleby)

who had been happy to use a Series III as an everyday commuter and weekend 'fun' car were beginning to realise that nimbler and easier-to-drive four-wheel vehicles might now be available.

On the other hand, the Land Rover enthusiast movement was gaining strength, and continued to do so with increasing force throughout the life of the Series III. There's little doubt that the more car-like qualities of the third generation Land Rover helped to bring people into Land Rover ownership but, at the same time, there was also a groundswell of interest in Series IIs and IIAs. Series Is became simultaneously even more popular as triallers, many being fitted with V8 engines, while others were drawn into the burgeoning classic car scene.

The final important event of the pre-coil-sprung Land Rovers was the introduction in February 1979 (but for overseas markets only) of the V8-powered 109-inch Series III, which was not available to British buyers until 1980. Known as the Stage 1 V8, this high-powered Series III was a direct result of massive Government investment in the then British Leyland Corporation under the Ryder Plan, and was a replacement for the six-cylinder model, whose engine had not been as successful as hoped.

The Stage 1 Land Rover showed the way

Solihull has known plenty of milestones. This photograph shows the factory celebration for the 250,000th model built. (James Taylor Collection)

forward, with the use of the Range Rover's permanent four-wheel drive and lockable centre differential, and it created a lot of interest with user groups who were desperately in need of more power than the four-cylinder engines could ever give, and better reliability under heavy-use conditions than the inlet-over-exhaust six-cylinder unit. It made an immediate impact in the 4x4 leisure market, especially in the highly attractive County Station Wagon form, and showed that Land Rover could compete – and beat – the rest of the world when it came to go-anywhere vehicles suitable to the new type of buyer.

Good though it was, however, the Stage 1 V8 did not lead directly to the first of the new generation of Land Rovers. Instead, all the lessons learned since 1948 with the utility vehicles, along with the technical developments which had made the Range Rover one of the world's most notable and successful 4x4s, would go into the melting pot from which an entirely new type of Land Rover would emerge in 1983.

Specifications

Dates are for model years.

Series I 80-inch (1948–54)

Engine (1948–51)	1,595cc IOE four-cylinder
Power	50bhp @ 4,000rpm
Torque	80lb/ft @ 2,000rpm
Engine (1952–4)	1,997cc IOE four-cylinder
Power	52bhp @ 4,000rpm
Torque	101lb/ft @ 1,500rpm
Transmission (1948–50)	Permanent four-wheel drive with front driveline freewheel; four-speed gearbox with transfer box
Transmission (1950–4)	Selectable four-wheel drive in high-ratios; permanent four-wheel drive in low; four-speed gearbox with transfer box
Steering	Recirculating ball, worm-and-nut system
Suspension	Live axles front and rear with semi-elliptic leaf springs and hydraulic dampers
Brakes	Hydraulic drums all round, with transmission parking brake
Dimensions	Wheelbase 80in (2.03m); track (front and rear) 50in (1.27m); length 123in (3.12m); width 61in (1.55m); height (1948–51) 70.5in (1.79m), (1951–4) 73.5in (1.87m)

Series I 86-inch (1954–6)

As for 80-inch except: wheelbase 86in (2.18m); length 140.7in (3.57m); width 62.6in (1.59m); height 76in (1.93m).

Series I 107-inch (1955–8)

As for 1954 80-inch except: wheelbase 107in (2.72m); length 173.5in (4.41m); width 62.6in (1.59m); height (basic model with hood) 83.5in (2.12m).

Series I 88-inch (1957–8)

As for post-1952 80-inch except: 2,052cc ohv four-cylinder diesel engine option with 51bhp @ 3,500rpm and 87lb/ft torque @ 2,000rpm; wheelbase 88in (2.23m); length 140.75in (3.57m); width 62.6in (1.59m); height 76in (1.93m).

Series I 109-inch (1957–8)

As for 88-inch except: wheelbase 109in (2.77m); length 173in (4.39m); height 83.5in (2.12m).

Series II 88-inch (1958–61)

Engine (petrol)	2,286cc ohv four-cylinder
Power	70bhp @ 4,250rpm
Torque	120lb/ft @ 2,500rpm
Engine (diesel)	As Series I
Transmission	As Series I
Suspension	As Series I
Brakes	As Series I
Dimensions	Wheelbase 88in (2.23m); track 51.5in (1.31m); length 142.4in (3.62m); width 64in (1.63m); height 77.5in (1.97m)

Series II 109-inch

As for 88-inch except: wheelbase 109in (2.77m); length 175in (4.44m); height 81in (2.06m).

Series IIA (1962–71)

Engine (petrol)	As Series II
Engine (diesel)	2,286cc ohv four-cylinder
Power	60bhp @ 4,000rpm
Torque	103lb/ft @ 1,800rpm
Transmission	As Series II
Suspension	As Series II
Brakes	As Series II
Dimensions	As Series II

Series IIA 109-inch

As for Series II 109-inch and, mechanically, Series IIA 88-inch except (from 1967): 2,625cc IOE six-cylinder engine option with 83bhp @ 4,500rpm and 128lb/ft torque @ 1,500rpm.

Series III 88-inch (1972–84)

As for Series IIA except: five-bearing crankshaft for four-cylinder engines from 1980; all-synchro gearbox.

Series III 109-inch

As for 88-inch; dimensions as Series IIA; six-cylinder engine discontinued in 1980.

Series III 109-inch V8 (1979–85)

As for standard 109-inch except: 3,528cc ohv V8 engine with 91bhp @ 3,500rpm and 166lb ft/torque @ 2,000rpm; permanent four-wheel drive with lockable centre differential.

Chapter **Three**

Birth of the One Ten and Ninety

A crucial step forward

It is true to say that Land Rover should have developed coil-sprung utility vehicles long before they did. The great success of the Range Rover was in no small part due to its extremely competent suspension and drive train, and there's no reason at all why Solihull's management should not have seen the way forward much earlier.

By the mid-1970s the Range Rover had

established itself, and had proved very quickly that the combination of low-rate, long-travel coil springs, permanent four-wheel drive, good brakes,

From the beginning, the Range Rover showed the way forward, yet traditionalism and the lack of a definite plan for the future development of the Land Rover, delayed the introduction of the luxury vehicle's mechanical and suspension advantages into the utility vehicles. (Nick Dimbleby)

and plenty of power was virtually unbeatable. Yet Land Rover felt constrained by the traditionalism of much of its market, particularly in developing countries, and by the resistance to change of its core United Kingdom agricultural market. Furthermore, throughout the 1970s the company's military customers around the world seemed more than happy with the Series III.

There was no carved-in-stone plan to replace the Series III, and the various experimental projects which were based on different versions of the Range Rover chassis and its suspension and running gear were largely half-hearted, and not all of them were what might be deemed official. True, there were reasons for not rushing into a new vehicle, but with hindsight most of these were more in the nature of excuses.

The entire Rover organisation has been afflicted at various times by spells of complacency, arrogance, and ignorance – sometimes simultaneously. This has also been true of Land Rover, albeit to a lesser extent, but has here applied more to certain key individuals at specific

periods rather than to Land Rover as a company.

Shortage of funds for investment in new vehicles is the reason usually trotted out to explain Land Rover's failure to bring out new models when, clearly, they have been needed. And, of course, it's true, because Land Rover was always having to prop up the parent company, which failed consistently in the post-war years to come up with cars which the general public wanted. Even the much-vaunted P6, excellent model that it was, wasn't able to generate sufficient cash to ensure future investment. Much of that burden was shouldered by Land Rover, just as it had been before and has been subsequently.

Despite that, the automotive world was moving on so rapidly by the mid-1960s that the Series III should have had only a short life, and maybe

As this prototype shot shows, the development of the One Ten avoided anything revolutionary as far as appearance was concerned. Indeed, by using Range Rover technology for the mechanical side of the new Land Rover, just about everything was tried and tested. (James Taylor Collection)

should never have existed at all. It was launched after the Range Rover and the fact that, firstly, it was actually introduced, and secondly, that it soldiered on until the mid-1980s, doesn't say much for Land Rover's planning. It's not unreasonable to point an accusing finger at Land Rover and ask why it was not ready to replace the Series IIA with the first generation of the Defender family by the mid to late 1970s, instead of coming up with the Series III which, other than its all-gear synchromesh, was little better than the IIA.

When they finally arrived, the One Ten and Ninety used the Range Rover's suspension and transmission, and variations on its chassis. Even the body was a reworking of that used for the Series IIA and III. If this was the correct answer in 1983 – and history has proved that it was – then it would also have been the right solution in the 1970s.

In the event, this is how it happened …

Mixed motivations

From the viewpoint of the British market, the introduction – let alone the development – of the fourth series of 'working' or utility Land Rovers was done in a manner which was difficult to understand. The short wheelbase version of the

then current Series III was by far the most popular with the principal users in the UK, who were somewhat mystified when the first of the coil-sprung generation was unveiled at the 1983 Geneva Motor Show.

There was an initial reaction among important user groups which didn't bode well for sales of the One Ten, as the new Land Rover was known. While those motoring journalists who had driven it wrote about it with enormous enthusiasm, and even those who had simply looked at it were glowing in their praise, Britain's farmers were not easily swayed by such opinions. They could not understand why the only wheelbase available was 110in (2.79m) when mostly they purchased short wheelbase models; they were perplexed that the same 2,286cc petrol and diesel engines which frustrated them in their Series IIIs had been carried over; and, generally speaking, were not taken in by the fact that they could have a 3.5-litre V8 if they wished.

But what this key sector of the home market didn't know, and probably would not have been impressed by even if they had, was that the decision to introduce the new vehicles with the long wheelbase version had been taken with the worldwide market in mind.

Land Rover was, of course, obliged to think globally – most of its export sales were currently 109-inch models – and not simply in terms of its principal UK buyers, and time has proved that the introduction of the coil-sprung Land Rovers was, indeed, done with the right models, which were destined to remain fundamentally unchanged for a very long time. However, that is not to say that the birth of the One Ten, followed a year later by the Ninety, was all part of a carefully laid-down marketing strategy within the corridors of power at Solihull. Indeed, it is no exaggeration to say that the story behind the introduction of coil springs to utility Land Rovers is a typical example (for Rover/Land Rover/British Leyland) of a catalogue of missed opportunities, dead ends, and pure chance, such as characterised the conglomerate into which Rover and Land Rover had been poured.

There was never a plan, as such, to replace the Series III with a completely new model at a particular point in time. It was more a case of it being obvious that a replacement would be needed, and that coil springing would have to be part of the package – or even the basis of it – and that more power was essential.

Part of the reason it happened the way it did was an acute shortage of cash for new Land Rover models, despite the soar-away success of the Range Rover. The make-or-break Rover SD1 car was scheduled for launch in 1976 and £27 million – then a massive amount – was to be poured into the project, including a new factory. Inevitably, this impacted heavily on Land Rover's intentions and actions in the middle years of the decade.

The Ryder Report of 1975 recommended huge investment in Land Rover vehicles, and one high-profile result was the first effort at modernising the 109-inch Series III by fitting it with the V8 as an option in 1979. Known as the Stage 1 because it represented the first stage in the investment programme, the resultant vehicle had a flat front (because of the positioning of the engine) and permanent four-wheel drive. However, it was not the direct antecedent of the One Ten as some observers have subsequently concluded.

It was the Range Rover rather than a utility Land Rover that showed the way forward, and in 1976 – three years before the Stage 1 came on the scene – a first prototype of a new-generation Land Rover

This photograph shows 100-inch prototype BAC 779T. The hoped-for large order from the Swiss Army failed to materialise and, after much deliberation, the idea of a 100-inch Land Rover was dropped. (James Taylor Collection)

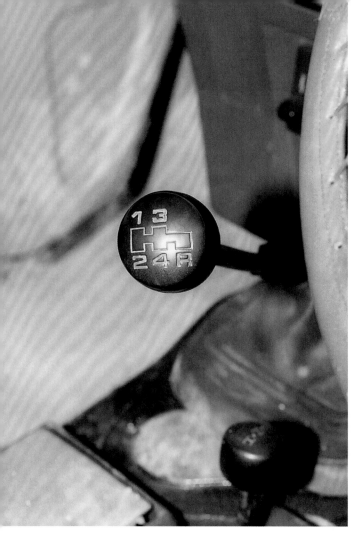

This is how it was for the first generation of One Ten V8s. Note the old Range Rover four-speed gearbox. All other One Tens had five gears, and although permanent four-wheel drive was standard, selectable four-wheel drive could be specified. Not many customers took that route however, and it was soon dropped. (Dave Barker)

DID YOU KNOW?

Stronger door

Because of the door-mounted spare wheel, a third hinge was added to the rear door of the Station Wagon for extra strength, with a higher mounting point for the wheel which hitherto had to be removed when towing.

DID YOU KNOW?

Air conditioning too

Among the options were fully integrated air conditioning and auxiliary fuel tanks, extending the standard capacity of 17.5gal (79.5l) to 27.5 (125l) or 32.5 (147.7l).

DID YOU KNOW?

Rainbow touch

Three new colours were introduced for the One Ten: Roan Brown, Trident Green, and Stratos Blue.

had been assembled using a standard 100-inch Range Rover chassis and a greatly cut-about Series III 109in body. The following year, another prototype was cobbled together – which is not a glib phrase, but a reflection of the way it actually happened – using a Range Rover chassis cut down from 100in (2.54m) to 90in (2.29m).

However, this V8-powered second prototype was seen essentially as a military vehicle, which it was hoped would replace the 88-inch Lightweight. But then the whole project was sideswiped by a decision to go back to a 100-inch plan, because it was hoped to produce an appropriate 100-inch chassis vehicle for an important order from the

Swiss Army. This deal never happened, but more than 70 100-inch prototypes were built before the idea of producing a Land Rover based on the standard Range Rover chassis was abandoned in 1986 – which was three years after the launch of the One Ten.

Common sense suggested otherwise, but Land Rover was still hankering for some form of 100-inch vehicle as a replacement for the 88-inch. But there was also the question of the 109-inch model. Would it remain as it was, but with a revised chassis design, or would it be wiser to make a fresh start? As it happened, there was already a 110-inch Range Rover chassis for ambulance conversions, and a 109-inch body, slightly modified, was mated with it in 1978, producing the very first version of the One Ten.

Development progressed, with Range Rover chassis characteristics very much to the fore, including the 5in (127mm) wider track – compared with the Series III – of the Range Rover's axles, which were given additional strength. The chassis itself was made a lot tougher, with deeper side members becoming its most noticeable characteristic. It was decided early on that the

Series III replacement would also feature permanent four-wheel drive.

The question of gearboxes, however, was not quite so straightforward. An excellent five-speed gearbox, the LT77, had been developed for the Rover SD1, but was not considered man enough for the V8 engine, especially with low ratios raising stress levels, leaving only the four-speed Range Rover unit (LT95) for the V8. Perhaps surprisingly, it was also decided to provide selectable four-wheel drive as an option with the diesel and four-cylinder petrol models. Maybe it was thought this would find favour with traditionalists.

As the project progressed and the One Ten took shape there were increasing misgivings about the 100-inch wheelbase idea, and Land Rover looked again at the once-abandoned 90-inch chassis for the short wheelbase model. So another prototype was built, again with a 90-inch axle-to-axle measurement.

Although 2in (50mm) longer than the 88-inch it was considered too short for the increasing demands being put on the very popular short wheelbase working machine, and was out-of-step with the (mainly Japanese) opposition. One more prototype was therefore assembled, but this time the chassis was stretched to 92.9in (2.36m) –

This impressive-looking machine is a 1983 One Ten County Station Wagon, registered CWK 37Y. The author owned an identical 1983 vehicle in the mid-1980s, but found the thirst of the V8 engine difficult to live with. (James Taylor Collection)

destined to become the production measurement. Because of the long time-gap between the very first 90-inch chassis and these two more recent ones, most people look on these as being 90-inch prototypes one and two.

With the wheelbases established there was now the question of styling. One major influence was the flat-front look of the Stage 1, which had to be retained in V8 versions because of the position of the engine, which in turn pushed the front ancillaries and radiator further forward; but it was a look which people liked. Another factor which contributed considerably to the final styling was the cost of the additional tooling which would be involved if the Series III body width was to be extended. Instead, deformable wheel arch eyebrows took care of the extra axle width.

The large one-piece windscreen, seat design, instrumentation, and various detail aspects came together with welcome smoothness, as did the pre-production programme, and the launch date was set. The Stage 2 Land Rover, representing the second stage of the investment programme which had begun with the Stage 1 V8, was on its way.

The new Land Rover

For the first time, the Land Rover stand was one of the principal features of the prestigious Geneva Motor Show in March 1983. The world's press always visit Geneva in strength, such is the importance of the event, and the star of the Solihull display, the first coil-sprung Land Rover, was one of the talking points around the show's halls and bars.

It was, for Land Rover, an historic event. Other than the Range Rover, the new vehicle was Solihull's first all-new model since the Series I, and although the One Ten's heritage was clearly evident in its styling – even to those with only a passing interest it could be nothing other than a Land Rover – its degree of innovation was described by some pundits as revolutionary.

Land Rover confirmed pre-Geneva announcements that the One Ten was to be sold first in Britain and Switzerland, followed by the rest of Europe, then the Middle East and the remainder of the world. It was not, as many had expected, an immediate replacement for the 88-inch and 109-inch Series IIIs which would, the company stated, remain in production for at least five more years.

The One Ten was available in five body types: soft-top, hardtop, pick-up, high capacity pick-up, and Station Wagon, plus a chassis cab for specialist conversions. The County Station Wagon variant, pioneered with the Series III, featured self-levelling rear suspension (optional on other models), cloth seats with head restraints, and tinted glass.

The One Ten's chassis was robot-built at Land Rover's Garrison Street factory, in which £7 million had been invested. It was based on the Range Rover frame, but strengthened as in the early prototypes, with a centre depth of more than 7.5in (190mm), and modified for the three engine options.

The coil springing produced a dramatic improvement in on-road ride comfort and a considerable boost in off-road performance through its much longer travel. With 7in (178mm) of vertical travel at the front and 8.25in (209mm) at the rear, suspension travel was up by 50 per cent and 25 per cent respectively. The gas-filled, oil-damped, self-energising Boge Hydromat rear strut was an important innovation, retaining full vertical movement of the rear coils, even under maximum load.

The Land Rover front beam axle was located by forged steel leading radius arms and a Panhard rod. The rear Salisbury axle was given tubular trailing links to control fore-and-aft movement, while an A-frame mounted centrally on the axle controlled lateral movement. Standard on the County Station Wagon was a rear-mounted anti-roll bar, carefully designed, according to Land Rover's engineering people, so as not to seriously restrict rear suspension travel.

The problem of braking shortcomings apparent on previous Land Rovers was addressed quite early in the development programme, and the new vehicle was given 11.8in (300mm) discs at the front and 11in (279mm) drums behind.

Power-assisted steering was listed as an option for the first time on a 'working' Land Rover; and although the company's traditional recirculating

Nearly three-quarters of all Land Rovers sold worldwide in the 1970s and early 1980s were long-wheelbase models, like this 109-inch, which is why Land Rover launched the One Ten before the Ninety. (Nick Dimbleby)

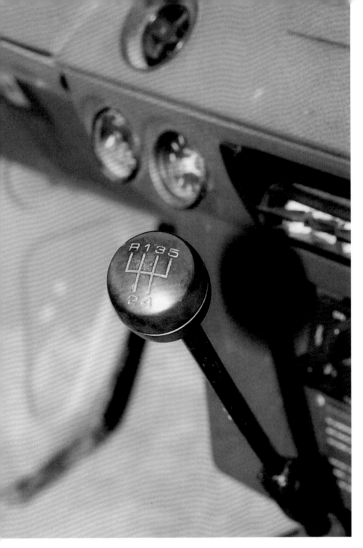

The adoption in 1985 of the five-speed gearbox for V8 models made a big difference to the Land Rover at cruising speed. This is the Range Rover version. (Dave Barker)

manual system on previous vehicles, giving a more modern way of stopping it.

Customers who wanted real power could opt for the familiar 3,528cc all-alloy Rover V8, which, although in a lower state of tune than in the Range Rover, gave 114bhp at 4,000rpm and a healthy 185lb/ft of torque at 2,500rpm. As with the Range Rover, there were two Zenith Stromberg CD carburettors.

The transmissions developed during the prototype period were unchanged. The new LT77 five-speed gearbox had been strengthened for use with the four-cylinder engines, while the V8 retained the now out-of-date four-speed LT95 'box from the Range Rover. It desperately needed an overdrive, but instead of being offered as a factory-fitted option it was only available as an aftermarket fitment from Fairey.

The five-speed gearbox was mated with the new, separate, LT230R transfer box, first used with the still-new automatic Range Rover, but the four-speed unit had the familiar integral transfer box from the manual Range Rover. With both gearboxes the transmission was the permanent four-wheel drive type with lockable centre differential (again from the Range Rover), but for those die-hards who wanted it there was also a Series III-type selectable four-wheel drive as an optional extra.

Enter the Ninety

Despite the popularity of the Series III (and before it the Series II and IIA) 88-inch in Britain, it was an inescapable fact that 70 per cent of Land Rovers sold worldwide in the early 1980s were long wheelbase versions – which is why Land Rover had no option but to introduce the One Ten first. But it was only a year before the second coil-sprung utility appeared, the 92.9in (2.36m) Ninety ... and already a number of changes had occurred.

Most important of these was the use of the newly developed 2.5-litre diesel engine. It took power up to 67bhp at 4,000rpm – still mediocre, but any improvement was worth having – while torque was now 114lb/ft at 1,800rpm.

The selectable 4x4 option was not offered on the new vehicle; virtually nobody had wanted it in One Ten form. And although you could still buy a One

ball system was retained, redesigned linkage made it lighter – even without assistance – and a lot more precise. The coil springs permitted a 5ft (1.5m) tighter turning circle than the 109-inch.

First engines

The familiar 2,286cc petrol and diesel engines were given a slight power boost for the One Ten. The petrol unit was improved with a revised camshaft, redesigned inlet and exhaust manifolds, and twin choke Weber 32/34 DMTL carburettor, although all this achieved was to take power from 70 to 74bhp at 4,000rpm. Diesel power was still unacceptably feeble, with only 60bhp at 4,000rpm and 103lb/ft of torque at 1,800rpm. But at least the diesel now had a solenoid cut-out in the ignition, rather than the

Ten with a V8 engine, the 3.5-litre unit was not available with the Ninety, even optionally, at the time of its launch.

The Ninety had Land Rover axles front and rear, without the option of a self-leveller, and without the One Ten County's anti-roll bar on the short wheelbase model's equivalent. Axle location and suspension arrangements were those pioneered the previous year, and there was the same power steering option.

On its introduction, the One Ten hadn't fully lost all traces of the vehicle it was destined to replace, because it had SIII-type sliding windows on the front doors. However, the Ninety came along with modern winding windows – but still without single-piece front doors – and these were installed in the One Ten at the same time. Body styles for the Ninety were shorter equivalents of the One Ten's, with the obvious exception of the high capacity pick-up only available with the longer wheelbase.

While the Ninety was received ecstatically by all who drove it, there was one reservation: the lack of a V8 meant that on-road performance and towing ability were restricted by the asthmatic and now ancient petrol engine and the still inadequate diesel. But just over a year after the Ninety's launch things began to happen, showing that Land Rover was indeed listening to its customers and was trying very hard to make its new vehicles the very best in all respects. In May 1985 the Ninety was given V8 power, the first time the 3.5-litre unit had been used in a short-wheelbase model, other than one which had been tried in the mid-1960s and a number of experimental 88-inch V8s in the 1970s. The Stage 1 V8, six years earlier, had been produced only with the 109-inch chassis. But now, the Ninety finally had the same high-power option as the One Ten, with ignition being upgraded to electronic type for better starting and more reliable tune.

The V8 gearbox was changed – at last – for the five-speed Santana-built LT85. Now both these mighty Land Rovers had a maximum speed better than 85mph (137kph), and could cruise all day at 75–80mph (120–128kph), provided you could afford the fuel. Consumption was a tad better than it had been with the four-speed gearbox on the One Ten,

but you were doing well to get 15mpg, and it could be as bad as 12mpg with a degree of enthusiasm.

Petrol engine changes didn't stop with the V8 Ninety, however. In the autumn of 1985 the four-cylinder petrol option for both vehicles changed to a 2,495cc derivative of the old petrol engine. It was, in fact, remarkably similar in many respects to the 2.5-litre diesel unit, introduced at the Ninety's launch, although it did not include the diesel's change-over from chain auxiliary drive to toothed belt. The power increase was welcome, with 83bhp at 4,000rpm, and 133lb/ft of torque at 2,000rpm.

With these improvements the new vehicles were well and truly on the motoring map. The four-cylinder engines now produced reasonable power, while word soon got around the important agricultural market in Britain that the coil springing really did make a significant difference to ride quality, and that much quieter running, even with the all-important (to farmers) diesel engine, meant you could hold a conversation at 50mph (80kph) – virtually impossible in a Series III diesel.

It had been very important for Land Rover to get the new utilities right before they went on the market, and this had been achieved, especially with the 2.5-litre four-cylinder engines. Importantly for many overseas markets, the traditional mechanical simplicity had been retained, facilitating servicing and even major repairs in remote locations and with a minimum of equipment.

Specifications

Land Rover One Ten (1983)

Engine	3,528cc petrol V8 overhead valve
	Bore/stroke: 88.9mm/71.7mm
	Compression ratio: 8.13:1
	Carburettors: Two Zenith Stromberg
Power	114bhp @ 4,000rpm
Torque	185lb/ft @ 2,500rpm
Steering	Recirculating ball with optional power assistance
Transmission	Four-speed permanent four-wheel drive with transfer box and lockable centre diff
Suspension	Front, beam axle with leading arms and Panhard rod, coil springs and telescopic dampers; rear, beam axle with trailing arms, central A-frame, coil springs, and telescopic dampers; self-levelling rear strut standard on County, optional on other models
Brakes	Front, 11.8in (300mm) discs; rear, 11in (279mm) drums; vacuum servo
Dimensions (County)	Wheelbase 110in (2.79m); track 58.5in (1.49m); length 180.3in (4.58m); width 70.5in (1.79m); height 80.1in (2.03m); ground clearance 8.5in (216mm); turning circle 42ft (12.81m); unladen weight 4,105lb (1,864kg); max payload 2,619lb (1,189kg)
Tyres	6.50 x 16 on 5.5in rims
Fuel capacity	17.5gal (79.5l)
Max speed	86mph (138kph)
0–60mph (0–96kph)	15.1sec
Consumption	12–17mpg

Other engines

	2,286cc petrol overhead valve
	Bore/stroke: 90.47mm/88.9mm
	Compression ratio: 8.0:1
	Carburettor: Weber 32/34 DMTL
Power	74bhp @ 4,000rpm
Torque	120lb/ft @ 2,000rpm
	2,286cc diesel indirect-injection overhead valve
	Bore/stroke: 90.47mm/88.9mm
	Compression ratio: 23:1
Power	60bhp @ 4,000rpm
Torque	103lb/ft @ 1,800rpm
Transmission	Five-speed permanent four-wheel drive (selectable 4x4 optional)

Land Rover Ninety (1984)

Engine	2,286cc petrol (as One Ten)
	2,495cc diesel indirect-injection overhead valve
	Bore/stroke: 90.47mm/97mm
	Compression ratio: 21:1
Power	67bhp @ 4,000rpm
Torque	114lb/ft @ 1,800rpm
Transmission	Five-speed permanent four-wheel drive (no selectable 4x4 option, which was also dropped on One Ten)

Remaining specifications as for One Ten except for following key points: rear brake drums 10in (254mm); tyres 6.00 x 16 or, on County, 205 x 16 radial; no self-leveller option; wheelbase 92.9in (2.36m); length 146.5in (3.72m); height 77.6in (1.97m) (CSW); fuel capacity 12gal (54.5l).

Key innovations

- First use of coil springs
- First of use of disc brakes
- First five-speed gearbox
- First use of self-leveller
- First one-piece windscreen
- First power-steering option

Chapter Four

The Defender arrives

Land Rover had no intention of standing still after the initial engine and transmission shortcomings of the new coil-sprung utilities had been rectified during the first couple of years. Customer feedback had identified some strongly felt demands for further improvement but, to be fair, Solihull's development people were very much on the ball and were working on a number of changes. Top of the list was the inadequacy of the 2.5-litre normally aspirated diesel engine, a long way short of the target where power was concerned. But there had also been comments about certain aspects affecting convenience and comfort. It has often been said that the One Ten and Ninety were given a post-launch facelift, and although this is perhaps an overstatement, the non-mechanical changes were nevertheless important.

Despite its upsizing to 2.5 litres in 1984, the diesel engine produced only 67bhp, a power figure at least a decade out of date when you consider the advances being made in diesel engines outside Land Rover. With a heavy load on board it made the performance of the One Ten in particular something of a joke; towing a heavy trailer, which is a task Land Rovers have always been designed for, meant extremely slow going, with much use of second and even first gear on hills. Land Rover's answer was to fit the Ninety and One Ten with a turbocharged development of the 2.5-litre diesel unit from October 1986, identifying models thus equipped with a rear-door badge proclaiming 'TURBO' for 1987 models, changing to 'turbo' for 1988. The full designation was Diesel Turbo.

DID YOU KNOW?

Air power

The air intake position for the Diesel Turbo models was unique. The intake grille was positioned high up in the left-hand side towards the front, between the top rear of the wheel arch eyebrow and the door pillar. This can be used to distinguish a Diesel Turbo model, even if it has subsequently been fitted with a different engine. (Many now have Tdi units.)

DID YOU KNOW?

3.9-litre diesel

Enthusiasm among Australians – always great fans of Land Rovers – for the early One Ten was aided greatly by the 3.9-litre diesel option, an attractive alternative to the V8, which was never offered in Britain. The engine was the Isuzu 4BD1 direct injection four-cylinder unit which, although no road-burner, produced 97bhp at 3,200rpm, some 50 per cent more than Land Rover's own diesel, and almost as much torque as the V8, its 188lb/ft coming at a very useful 1,800rpm.

In 1986 the 3.9 diesel was given the same five-speed gearbox as the V8, with identical ratios other than lower overall gearing in the high-range transfer. The main gearbox ratios suited the diesel much less than it did the V8, and the first four gears were much the same as they had been before the new gearbox. Fifth, however, became a genuine overdrive, much appreciated on some of Australia's never-ending, dead straight outback roads.

During the last few years before the introduction of the Defender name, Land Rover was improving the vehicles consistently, but before the Tdi was available no significant upgrade was possible. (Nick Dimbleby)

Using the code name Project Falcon, this engine had been under development for two years before its introduction at the end of 1986, and was part of a general engine improvement programme. Although it has become fashionable in recent years to criticise this original turbo diesel – much of the adverse comment coming from people unable to look at it from the perspective of 1986 – its introduction was a turning point of great significance for Land Rover. As we now know, it turned out to be a stop-gap engine presaging the introduction of the much-improved 200 Tdi. But although Land Rover knew it would have to come up with an altogether better engine as a long-term solution to its general diesel shortcomings, when the Diesel Turbo went into production it was not known how long it would have to be used and precisely what would replace it.

Project Gemini, which was to lead to the 200 Tdi, had begun several months after the instigation of Project Falcon towards the end of 1984. The principal driving force behind Gemini, of course, was to come up with a world-class diesel for all of Solihull's vehicles, but, right up to the point just prior to it going into production, there remained a strong lobby within Rover for a bought-in turbocharged diesel engine; not everybody had the confidence that Land Rover was capable of developing a new-generation power unit.

Stop-gap it may have been, but contrary to a widely held notion, the 2.5-litre Diesel Turbo introduced in late 1986 was not a bolt-on conversion. True, the new engine was based on the existing 2.5-litre unit, itself only introduced at the end of 1983, but considerable research and re-engineering lay behind it. Land Rover had developed a new cylinder block with integral turbocharger oil feed and drain, along with a revised crankshaft which had been given cross drillings in order to improve the lubrication of the bearing journals. The company had also introduced completely new pistons and piston

rings, while nimonic exhaust valves were used to cope with the much higher combustion temperatures associated with turbocharging.

For the turbocharger, Land Rover had gone to Garrett. The unit used with the new engine was the AiResearch T2, with an integral wastegate limited to 10psi. Diesel injection was with a DPS self-priming pump with boost control capsule and cold start timing retard system.

Because of the increased temperatures, along with the additional power output, the cooling system was uprated from that used in pre-turbo vehicles. In part this was accomplished with a standard-fitment oil cooler, but the viscous fan was improved and new heat shielding developed.

Much of the work during the development of the new engine had concentrated on improving bottom-end torque and minimising turbo lag. It

This badge proclaimed Land Rover's first turbocharged diesel engine, the 2.5-litre Diesel Turbo. The name was used in this way to avoid confusion with the VM-powered Range Rover. (James Tayor Collection)

Usually, only visitors to motor shows get the chance to see Land Rovers like this! The picture demonstrates clearly the tough construction of the chassis, and the suspension layout. (Nick Dimbleby)

certainly paid off, because the new engine produced 85bhp at 4,000rpm (the old engine gave 67bhp). More importantly for a working, off-roading 4x4, the torque figure was improved from 114lb/ft to 150lb/ft, but still at 1,800rpm.

Important for many of Land Rover's export customers was the fact that the new engine would run perfectly well on very low cetane numbers (as low as 4C), and would perform well at high altitude.

The effect of this engine development work could be felt immediately you opened the throttle. For the first time a diesel-powered Land Rover had reasonable acceleration and acceptable maximum (75mph, or 121kph) and cruising speeds. With the aerodynamics of a brick, neither the Ninety nor the One Ten could ever be a road-burner, but the new engine gave the Ninety a 0–60mph (0–96kph) acceleration time of a touch over 22 seconds. Not

DID YOU KNOW?

Ninety or 90?

In the run-up to the introduction of the Defender name Land Rover ceased referring to the Ninety and One Ten during 1989 and instead called them the 90 and 110. It is therefore technically correct to refer to 1989 model year vehicles by their spelled-out names, but to use the figures 90 and 110 for models produced from 1990 onwards.

DID YOU KNOW?

Two turbo diesels

Land Rover chose to use the name Diesel Turbo, instead of Turbo Diesel, for the 1986 launch of their turbo-charged utility vehicles in order to avoid confusion which might have arisen with the VM-powered diesel Range Rover, known as the Turbo D.

For 1988 Defenders the dash was redesigned, giving the radio (where fitted) a far more suitable position. (James Taylor Collection)

The Station Wagon variant of the One Ten and Ninety was a very attractive vehicle, as this pre-Defender photograph shows and its popularity increased markedly in later years. (Nick Dimbleby)

Porsche-like, it's true, but compare this with the V8 Ninety's 0–60mph time of 14.2 seconds, and maximum speed of 83mph (133kph). Better still, look at the 29 seconds achieved by the four-cylinder petrol version of the Series III.

The 1986 Motor Show was also the platform for other important improvements to the Ninety and One Ten. Until now the utility vehicle V8 engines had continued to use carburettors, whereas the Range Rover had gone over to fuel injection, which took power to 165bhp. For the 1987 model year the switch was made from twin Strombergs to a pair of SUs and this, along with a new camshaft, took the power output to 134bhp – more, incidentally, than Range Rover V8s had been producing before their switch to injection. The increase in performance was welcomed by customers, although they still had to contend with high fuel consumption. The V8 is a thirsty unit, particularly so when used with the Ninety and One Ten, and there was nothing of significance to be done about it.

Apart from an important switch to new one-

piece doors, other changes didn't amount to very much. However, one particularly sensible modification was the relocation of the radio panel, from just in front of the gear lever to a recessed position in the centre of the fascia. This spelled the end of channel changing whenever you swapped gears, although it took away a chunk of already sparse oddments space.

Door trims were improved, along with locking buttons and door handles, a new filler cap, and County Station Wagons were given a fresh set of decals, the third since launch. The Ninety County was given enamelled five-spoke Rostyle wheels, giving it a less utilitarian appearance.

The changes for the 1988 model year were mostly cosmetic, perhaps the biggest surprise being that the 'new' models were shown, not at the traditional Motor Show (more correctly the London Motorfair), but in December at the Royal Smithfield Show. Much of the emphasis in this late 1987 exhibition was on the County Station Wagons, which Land Rover wanted to popularise as much as possible in advance of the launch of the Discovery, scheduled for the autumn of 1989. It was obvious that the forthcoming vehicle would attract some buyers who would otherwise choose

the County Station Wagon, so it made sense to make the CSW as attractive as possible.

The 1988 models became the first Land Rovers ever to depart from the traditional galvanised finish for the bumpers, in favour of black paint. On County Station Wagons the black bumper – which looked very strange at first – was complemented with body-colour grille, headlamp surrounds, and wheel arch eyebrows. On other models these parts were black. The County set also gained yet another side decal design and, far more usefully, a new type of Britax sunroof, offered as an extra on other models. Interiors became a little more car-like with revised trim, and there were better window seals.

Smithfield was again chosen the following year to announce the 1989 models, but the changes were few, with much fiddling of decals once more, and Rostyle wheels becoming an all-model option within the Ninety range (they were already standard on the County Station Wagons). Most noticeable was the redesign of the upper body sides for hardtops and Station Wagons, on which the rivet heads were no longer exposed. This certainly made the County types more visually appealing.

Not much happened the following year either, although the adoption of the now-familiar green oval Land Rover badge in its position on the radiator grille brightened the front somewhat. The plate above the grille was now without the Land Rover name, instead simply reading '90' or '110'.

The most important aspect of these 1990 models was that they were the last Land Rovers not to have a separate name. Since the inception of the marque in 1948 all utility models had been known simply as Land Rovers, but this was about to change for good – causing no little controversy along the way.

Defender was about to arrive.

The 127

It is often forgotten that the 127 dates back as far as the One Ten – or rather the designation does, because it was the end of 1983, rather than the

spring, when the extra-long-wheelbase variant first became available.

The Special Projects department started considering the One Ten as the basis for special conversions, principally by authorised aftermarket conversion companies, shortly before the official launch of the coil-sprung Land Rover. At about the same time it was noted that there ought to be a market for a model with a high-capacity pick-up rear body and a four-door, five-man cab up front, and it was put to Special Projects that the way forward would be to produce the vehicle with a special, 135-inch chassis.

There was no problem in constructing a cab but, because the suggested extra-long chassis was not a viable proposition, it ended up as a 127-inch derivative of the One Ten frame carrying a shortened version of the rear body for the normal

After the 1989 models, the company decided not to display the Land Rover name on the plate above the grille, anticipating the full switch to Defender, which was announced at the 1990 Motor Show. (Nick Dimbleby)

Starting as the 127, the extra-long-wheelbase pick-up evolved into the 130, coincidental with the adoption of the Defender name. Despite the numbers, the wheelbase remained the same; these vehicles were initially hand-converted from 110 chassis, switching to the production line with the start of Defender. (Nick Dimbleby)

Four box body variations of the 127/130 were produced, offering customers the choice of short or long body (depending on whether the normal or Crew Cab was used), with tall or short sides. Further special variations have been built by companies such as Foley Specialist Vehicles. (Nick Dimbleby)

high-capacity pick-up. It was called the Crew Cab.

Up to mid-1985, all production vehicles were hand-converted from standard One Ten chassis by Solihull's Special Projects department. This was not the way things had been done in the past, when companies such as Spencer Abbott would have been responsible for production versions of vehicles such as the Crew Cab – but it was the way it would work from now on.

Under the dynamic managing directorship of Tony Gilroy, Land Rover was becoming much more cost-conscious and profit minded. One effect of this was the reorganisation of Special Projects into a new division known as Special Vehicle Operations. It was part of SVO's job to take back in-house much of the hitherto farmed-out aftermarket conversion work, and it was within this new regime that the original Crew Cab spawned a complete family of vehicles based on the 127-inch chassis. From the second half of 1985 they would be badged as the Land Rover 127.

As well as the 127 Crew Cab, SVO also developed many other variations of the basic box body. With four variations to the basic body – short or long

This is the badge of the Range Rover Turbo D from which Land Rover was obliged to differentiate with the name of the Diesel Turbo Ninety and One Ten. (James Taylor Collection)

(depending on whether or not it was to be used with the Crew Cab) and high or low – it was not at all difficult for Land Rover to produce just about anything customers wanted for military or civilian use.

When the original One Ten and Ninety became Defender 110 and 90 the SVO 127 was renamed the Defender 130. This was not because, as some owners had thought at the time, there was any increase in wheelbase; it was simply the result of an understandable desire to have nice, easy numbers throughout the whole family of utility vehicles.

At the same time, output of all 127-inch vehicles was switched to the production line, providing more economical build for this increasingly popular variant and, at the same time, giving a bit of welcome elbow room within SVO – which was renamed again in 1992, when it became Land Rover Special Vehicles.

Chapter **Five**

The Defender: Tdi to Td5

Before the arrival of the Discovery in September 1989, any suggestion that a 'working' Land Rover might have a name all its own would have seemed as far-fetched as Land Rover Ltd being able to produce a world-beating diesel engine. The Discovery dispelled any fears about the diesel engine … but what about the idea that a Land Rover might be called something other than a Land Rover?

There were two very good reasons for introducing a name for the utility models. With only a two-vehicle range prior to the Discovery – Land Rover and Range Rover – names hadn't mattered a great deal, but in the run-up to the Discovery's introduction the marketing people felt compelled to find a suitable label for the Ninety and One Ten. It would avoid confusion and tie everything down rather neatly.

The second point they had to consider was the high value of the Land Rover name as a notable motoring marque. The company name, therefore, would be much better reserved for use in its corporate sense, and, regardless of other considerations, this meant that it would no longer be acceptable for a vehicle produced by Land Rover Ltd to be known as, simply, a Land Rover.

In naming the utility range Defender, Land Rover broke the no-model-name tradition which had stood since 1948. The choice of such a military-sounding name caused an outcry for a month or so, but the world soon became accustomed to it, and it is now difficult to think of calling these vehicles anything else. (Nick Dimbleby)

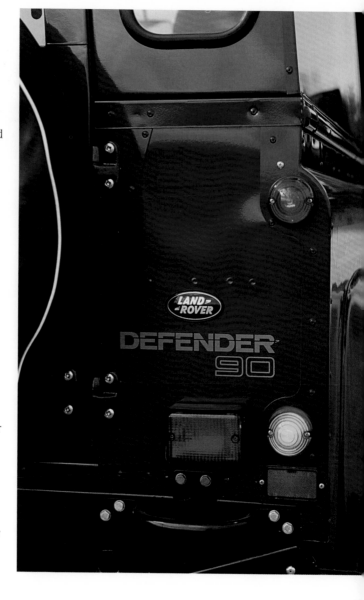

Several explanations have been given for the use of the Defender name. Land Rover said at the time that the alternative was Attacker, and it was also stated that Defender 'came from nowhere' during a session in a Boston bar involving visitors from head office and their North American subsidiary hosts. It's neither clear how many 'possibles' were listed, nor is it known whether there were any serious misgivings at Land Rover about the new name.

Defender was catapulted into the public eye at

The 300 Tdi engine succeeded the 200 Tdi, which was launched in 1989. Both these 2.5-litre turbocharged, direct injection units were world beaters and remain in many ways the best off-roading power units ever constructed. (Nick Dimbleby)

the Birmingham International Motor Show in September 1990. I was there on Press Day with the rest of the media and recall clearly the surprise expressed at the choice of name, the real joy at the use of the 200 Tdi diesel engine in the 'working' vehicle range … and the indifference to the modest list of other improvements.

Exteriors were decked out in bright decals, making much of the Defender name, but were otherwise very much 'as you were'. Inside, there was at last a cubby box available between the outer pair of front seats, which had each been moved inboard an inch to give more elbow room, and cloth seat coverings were now an option. Land Rover also tried to excite visitors with the news that courtesy lights had at last been fitted to a utility Land Rover and the wash-wipe programme had been improved.

However, compared with the importance of the new engine, and what at the time seemed a strange choice of name, it would have taken a major internal makeover to arouse any real interest. Those who knew their Land Rovers were pleased that the old LT85 Santana gearbox had been replaced with a revised version of the LT77, specially strengthened for the V8 and therefore possessing more than adequate reserves for the new diesel. However, it was the Tdi we all wanted to talk about.

This engine had already been used in the Discovery for a year before it first appeared in the Defender, and had received nothing but praise from motoring writers and users alike. Most importantly it had proved reliable, although some problems

Responding to a growing interest in 'lifestyle' motoring, Land Rover produced the Cariba concept vehicle in the 1980s, picking up the theme with the introduction of the 90SV in 1993. (James Taylor Collection)

would develop as time marched on, and it was without doubt a major factor in the Discovery's amazing first-year success story. It was not, however, an engine which had been developed especially for the Discovery and then shifted over

This is the 300 Tdi Defender. Although the engine retained the same power and torque characteristics of the 200 Tdi, it was substantially re-engineered, and was significantly quieter and smoother. A revised gearbox, the R380, was introduced with the new engine. (Nick Dimbleby)

to the Defender production line in order to give the utilities the benefits of Discovery's engine. As my description of the development of the Tdi (below) shows, one of the factors behind the project which led to the Tdi was the absolute necessity for Land Rover to have a top-flight diesel in order to be able to make an impact on European markets – which were diesel dominated – with the 'working' models.

The Tdi exceeded all expectations, and it was an enormous achievement that a company the size of Land Rover, a very small player in the big boy's world of car manufacture, was able to produce a diesel engine not bettered by anything in its class. It transformed the 90 and 110, and probably averted serious difficulties at Land Rover. Market conditions, which included real competition for the Station Wagons from the Discovery, and the excellent qualities of the Toyota Hi-Lux pick-up truck, which made it a genuine 'working' vehicle competitor, led to falling sales throughout the early 1990s. Without the Tdi engine it is practically certain that the Defender would have been in

trouble. In its Defender application the Tdi was nevertheless given less power and torque than the Discovery: 107bhp at 3,800rpm and 188lb/ft at 1,800rpm.

Very little happened over the next few years, with changes restricted to detail in the brake systems and a different steering wheel. One improvement appreciated by drivers, though, was the better gear selection with the LT77S gearbox introduced in 1992 models.

Solihull caused a stir in 1993 when it introduced its first addition to the Defender range in the shape of the 90SV, aimed squarely at the market for weekend fun vehicles. It picked up the theme of the Cariba, a concept vehicle which the company had played around with some six years earlier, and was a glamorised pick-up with County cab, a full roll cage, other 'lifestyle' adornments, and no choice of engine. It was the Tdi or nothing!

For 1996 the Defender was given Freestyle wheels, although as an optional extra, improving the vehicle's appearance and adding to the 'lifestyle' appeal. (Nick Dimbleby)

The 90SV ('SV' standing for Special Vehicles) was built exclusively for the home market, with no left-hand drive option, and could have been far more popular than it was. But the conversion from standard pick-up was done, one-at-a-time, by the Special Vehicles department, which kept the price up and numbers down. Much was made of the 90SV having disc brakes all-round, instead of the Defender's system hitherto of discs at the front and drums at the rear. However, this now became standard on all Defenders, the harmonisation of braking arrangements with the Discovery making good sense for Land Rover, and even better sense for its customers.

At the same time as the 90SV was launched, the seven-seat County Station Wagon was reintroduced, making a particularly attractive version of the 90, although the desperate lack of space when all seven seats were occupied reduced its practicality somewhat. There was room for three more in the new ten-seat 110 County Station Wagon, while the 12-seater continued as before.

Defenders took another important step forward in March 1994 when several key changes were announced, some of which affected all vehicles in the Solihull line-up. The central theme was a new diesel engine. Although the 200 Tdi had been well-received and was genuinely a world-beating engine, it had its shortcomings. For a start it was noisy, although when compared with its Diesel Turbo predecessor it was remarkably refined. While its hard-sounding beat was a characteristic of direct injection diesels, it had been decided at an early stage that the original unit needed improving. Some reliability problems had developed as well, further justifying development work.

The engine revealed in the spring of 1994 was much more than a simple revision of the original Tdi. Its name, the 300 Tdi, was simply a marketing label because there was no change in capacity, no increase in power or torque, and no change in the

The Defender XD, or Wolf, was a specially strengthened version which rapidly became a favourite with a number of military customers. More than 8,000 are in service with the British forces. (Nick Dimbleby)

basic philosophy of the 200 Tdi. However, a great deal of work had been done, resulting in 208 new components, many of them fundamental to the operation of the engine. These included cylinder head, exhaust manifold, turbocharger, injectors, pistons, conrods, timing belt, alternator, and water pump.

The result was astonishing, especially to the thousands of everyday users who had been more than happy with the first Tdi. The new engine was a much neater installation, a great deal smoother, and noticeably quieter, and while it couldn't make the diesel-powered Defender as civilised as a V8, the difference now was much less than anyone who had driven an original One Ten back in 1983 would have believed possible.

Along with the new engine – fitted to Discoverys and Range Rovers in exactly the same tune – was a new gearbox, the R380, which gave smoother and slicker changes, had synchromesh on reverse, and a revised double-H gate. Also making life easier

was a reworked clutch mechanism which reduced the pedal operating pressure to acceptable levels at last.

The Defender, an excellent vehicle from the beginning, was now unbelievably good. With the introduction of the 300 Tdi engine its usefulness as an everyday car, even for people with very long commuting journeys, was beyond doubt. In County form, especially as a 110, it was a serious rival even for the company's own Discovery. It only required a look around any supermarket car park to see just how popular it was becoming as a non-working utility vehicle.

The trend in this direction continued with 1996 models, when front and rear anti-roll bars were offered as options, along with Freestyle wheels and

The Defender V8 50 was produced as a limited-edition model in celebration of Land Rover's 50th anniversary. It featured a 4-litre fuel-injected V8 and, for the first time in a UK production model, automatic transmission. (Nick Dimbleby)

BF Goodrich All Terrain tyres. In part this was due to requirements for the NAS (North American Specification) vehicles. NAS influence could also be seen in a special-edition 300 Tdi 90, the Defender 90 Eastnor, produced for the French market.

During this model year, Land Rover won a most important military order for the Defender XD, or Wolf, which not only stamped the seal of approval on the Defender from the most demanding of all users, but also did more than anything else to guarantee its continued existence. The British MoD contracted for 8,800 vehicles, and this in turn sparked off orders from other countries.

Improvements for 1997 and 1998 were restricted to detail and to the choice of wheels, with interior trim receiving even more attention; and with 1998 being Land Rover's 50th anniversary year, it was no great surprise to find Collectors' Edition vehicles for all model ranges, Defender's allocation being the Defender V8 50, introduced in June. Based very much on American model policy, this was a 90 County Station Wagon with 4-litre injected V8, ZF automatic transmission, and full external roll cage. Air conditioning was standard and there was considerable attention to external

The Defender Td5, with five-cylinder direct injection turbo diesel engine, represents a technological step forward. However, the degree of electronic sophistication is an unknown quantity when it comes to severe off-roading, and the vehicle's use in remote, Third-World territories. (Nick Dimbleby)

and internal trim – without doubt, the best pre-Td5 Defender to be built.

And, yes, the new-breed Defender was waiting in the wings, because with the 1998 models the first series of Defenders had run its course. Enthusiasts throughout the world held their breath.

The Defender Td5

The first new Defender since the advent of the Tdi engine represents a great technical advance over the old Defender, but the electronic nature of these advances is causing concern among some user groups.

The Td5 looks very much like any other recent Defender – indeed, only an enthusiast would spot the tiny air vents between the front sidelights and direction indicators and the elongated indicator repeaters – but the differences are huge. Most important is the introduction of the five-cylinder direct injection diesel engine, another triumph of engineering for Solihull and an enormous step forward in terms of power, torque, and refinement compared with the 300 Tdi. It produces 122bhp at 4,200rpm, a useful increase over the Tdi, and 195lb/ft of torque at 1,950rpm compared with 188lb/ft at 1800rpm.

The Td5 is very much an engine of the 21st century, and is set to provide diesel power for Solihull vehicles for many years to come. It is fully monitored and controlled by an electronic control unit (ECU), and there is electronically controlled injection by individual camshaft-driven pumps for each cylinder. There is also an electronic system to improve the match of engine speed and drive train speed, reducing the onset of shunt and snatch, further assisted with a new type of dual-mass flywheel.

The throttle pedal travel is short for an off-road vehicle, in which reasonably long travel is usually required to obtain smooth operation in low ratios. With the Td5 the engine management system adjusts the tune of the engine when low range is selected, changing the response of the engine to throttle action and electronically 'elongating' the action.

All these features are standard. As options you can also have Land Rover's excellent ABS system – one of the very few to have full off-road effectiveness – and electronic traction control (ETC), which operates in conjunction with the ABS. With these fitted, the Defender's traction is unbelievably good over all forms of terrain, permitting it to maintain traction when only one wheel is gripping, something you can otherwise only achieve with locking differentials on both axles used in conjunction with a centre diff lock.

The Td5 has also been brought up to date with revised instrumentation, which includes a very

The engine bay of the Defender Td5 is a far cry from the cluttered, untidy appearance of the original turbocharged diesel engine, the Diesel Turbo. The five-cylinder engine is the smoothest ever Land Rover diesel unit. (Dave Barker)

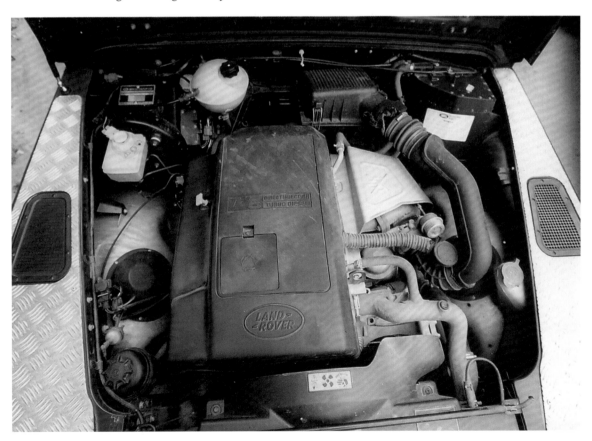

useful 'water in fuel' indicator, giving advance warning of diesel degradation. There's better seat trim and improved sound insulation too.

Clearly, the latest Defender is the best so far – but only as long as the electronics can take the punishment which is inevitable when the world's best off-roader is used to its limits.

Tdi development

Long before the Defender was planned, Land Rover had known it would have to do something about its diesel engine. There was a project to produce a diesel version of the V8 (Iceberg, aborted in late 1983). This was followed by Project Falcon, which was to turbocharge the existing diesel, newly enlarged to 2.5 litres, and there was also Project Beaver, in which the 2.4-litre Italian VM unit would be fitted to the Range Rover.

The Falcon engine was announced in October 1986 and was warmly received; and, of course, the VM unit was fitted to the Range Rover, but without

Land Rover beat the rest of the world with the 200 Tdi, which was the first small-capacity direct injection diesel (compared with truck engines) to go into mass production. It was a much more suitable engine for the various 4x4 applications at Solihull than anything from the opposition. (Dave Barker)

the resounding success a better engine would have enjoyed. Both projects had, anyway, been viewed as short-term solutions.

The really important project was Gemini, which commenced in the early part of 1985. This was the key part of the strategy being developed by powertrain chief John Bilton, who was convinced that the way forward in the European 4x4 market was with a new generation of diesel engines. He knew that Ford, Audi, and Fiat were working on small-capacity direct injection units (a system hitherto popular only with HGV engines). He knew, too, that direct injection for car (and 4x4) use was by no means proven, but nevertheless took a gamble by selecting this as the way forward for Gemini.

Although the fuel economy benefits of direct

injection were well proven, so too was the much greater combustion noise and lack of refinement. However, Bilton knew that work on two-spring, or dual-rate, injection was being carried out by both Bosch and by Lucas/CAV. He thought that this was where the breakthrough would come. Eventually, Land Rover opted for the Bosch injection system for what was to become the 200 Tdi, although Lucas/CAV had also figured prominently in the development programme.

The two-spring Bosch system provides a rising-rate return spring for the injectors. This slows the initial rate of injection and controls the rate of rise of combustion pressure, which has a significant effect on diesel 'knock', particularly on start-up, always the bugbear of the direct system. But the new engine would not work as a high-revving (in diesel terms) car power unit without a considerable re-think on the combustion chambers, compared with the design currently employed by Land Rover.

To sort this out, Bilton went to AVL in Graz, Austria, at the time the world's leading diesel

For many years, the One Ten was a mainstay machine for the British Ministry of Defence, just as the Defender has been. The normally aspirated version of the 2.5 diesel engine virtually pioneered the use of diesel for Land Rovers used by the British armed forces. (Nick Dimbleby)

consultants, and way ahead of the game in direct injection technology and know-how. AVL gave Land Rover what was needed to make the combustion process work as required, and were also extensively involved in improving reliability and durability.

Development work was carried out at Solihull. The new engine shared the dimensions of the then existing 2.5-litre turbo diesel, around which it was generally based. But it was given a new block, pistons, and conrods, and the direction of water flow through the block was reversed, although, interestingly, it was able to be machined on the same line as the existing (pre-Tdi) unit. The Diesel Turbo's crankshaft was retained – just about the only component which was – although the cold rolling process was improved. The most dramatic change was in the cylinder head, cast in aluminium alloy and produced in a completely new CNC (computerised numerical-controlled) machining centre. The straightforward two valves per cylinder, pushrod operated system was retained.

Overall, the engine was 45lb (20kg) lighter than the turbo diesel. It produced virtually the same power, and more torque at lower rpm, than the VM then being used in the Range Rover, and it was apparent that this unit would, indeed, be suitable across the range, as had been the intention all along.

Turbocharging experience gained with the Diesel Turbo proved invaluable, although it was a long time before the development team was satisfied it had a set-up capable of producing the desired power/torque/reliability characteristics. In the event, the Garrett T25 turbocharger, coupled with an efficient intercooler, proved capable of doing the job remarkably well.

More than two million test miles were put into the new engine in all manner of vehicles, and history has endorsed it as one of the British motor industry's more significant engines.

It was only nine months before the launch of the Discovery in 1989 that it was finally decided to use the Gemini engine for this vehicle and, subsequently, in all diesel-powered Solihull models. As John Bilton said at the time, 'There was a lot of pressure during the development of the 200 Tdi to opt for a bought-in engine.'

Military models

The One Ten went into military service in Britain in 1985, closely followed by the Ninety and then, after a while, the 127. The first overseas military order came from Holland in 1984.

Diesel power for the British forces was pioneered by the One Ten with the 2.5-litre normally aspirated diesel, and diesel subsequently becoming a near-standard type of engine for

A number of Ninetys were used by British forces in the Gulf War; because they were in some ways scaled-down versions of the famed Pink Panthers (109-inch vehicles nicknamed 'Pinkies') it was not surprising the Ninetys were dubbed 'Dinkies'. (Nick Dimbleby)

British military Land Rovers.

The most common form of the One Ten in the British forces was always the soft-top, and a GS (General Service) version was the first to be developed at Solihull. Other types rapidly followed, including the Shortland armoured car variant along with other armoured bodies, often to special order.

A notable development on the basic One Ten during the 1980s was the DPV (Desert Patrol Vehicle) to replace the SAS Pink Panthers, while the 1990s saw the production of the V8-powered SOV (Special Operations Vehicle) for the US Rangers. This came about from the Americans seeing Land Rovers in action during the Gulf War, and deciding that they'd like their own.

The Ninety, with its reduced load-carrying capacity, has been much less popular with the world's armed forces. Many observers thought it would take over from the Series III Lightweight for airborne operations but, in fact, the One Ten largely assumed those duties. That's not to say

Ninetys have not seen service, because considerable numbers have been ordered for communications and other duties not requiring the carrying capability of the One Ten. Most, but not all, military Ninetys have been hardtops. The Land Rovers which so inspired the Americans during the Gulf War were diesel Ninetys, rapidly converted into scaled-down versions of the Series IIA Pink Panthers, and instantly dubbed 'Dinkies' by the squaddies who used them.

However, the Defender series saw the re-emergence of the short-wheelbase Land Rover as a fighting machine alongside the 110 and 130, as a result of Project Wolf, in which a new breed of military 4x4 was developed. The first vehicles were

The Wolf, or Defender XD, had to be given a much stronger chassis, tougher body-to-chassis mountings and a detachable roll cage before it was acceptable to the Ministry of Defence. Mechanically, these Land Rovers are as near-standard as possible, something which has characterised military Land Rovers throughout the company's history. (Nick Dimbleby)

provided for battlefield trials in 1993, following which modified and strengthened second-generation Wolf vehicles were eventually ordered at the beginning of 1996. Land Rover decided these tougher-than-usual variants should have a name, and they settled on Defender XD (eXtra Duty), otherwise known as the Wolf. They have subsequently proved extremely popular around the world.

A great deal of work went into developing these special military Defenders. They have stronger chassis, tougher body-to-chassis mountings, reinforced body, and removable roll cage over the rear body. Although they have been kept as standard as possible mechanically, XDs have a tougher rear axle and four-pinion differential to cope with the extra loading.

The Wolf, or XD, is extremely popular with its users, especially those whose job it is to drive them and fight with them. The product of entirely fresh thinking at Solihull regarding military Land Rovers, it has ensured the continuation of a fine tradition

North American Specification (NAS) Defenders have always featured a number of differences compared with those destined for the European market. They have all been powered by the V8 petrol engine although, with the introduction of the Td5 at the end of 1998, American customers have had to accept diesel power. (Nick Dimbleby)

DID YOU KNOW?

Goodbye V8

Over the years Land Rover has phased out the V8 engine from its utility models, first by reducing the number of models with which it could be specified, then eliminating it altogether from the 90 and, finally, the 110.

Except by placing a special order it has otherwise been impossible to buy a V8, partly because the Tdi provided to be a genuine alternative, but much more because Land Rover wished to simplify production as much as possible. While it is fair to say that orders for V8s were in decline before the introduction of the 200 Tdi, many customers felt strongly that they should have been offered the choice. After the V8 was dropped from the 90 line-up altogether, many buyers who had wanted a V8 90 switched to 110s with the big petrol engine, even though they did not necessarily want the long wheelbase.

Interestingly, Land Rover chose the 4-litre version of the V8 for the Defender 50 limited edition in 1998, because they wanted to produce a special vehicle with the greatest-possible appeal!

of manufacturing vehicles for defence and police forces around the globe.

The Defender in the USA

Although the Discovery proved popular in the USA, it was important for Land Rover to sell Defenders as well in order to enforce the company's heritage and image. NAS Defenders gradually improved in specification and safety features – such as air bags and roll cages in order to comply with Federal regulations – and were all V8-powered, progressing to the 3.9-litre injected version of the long-lived ex-Buick engine in 1995.

For 1997 the specifications were upgraded for the last time. These models were given the 4-litre version with GEMS engine management and OBD II on-board diagnostics, but their most significant feature was that they became the first of Solihull's utility vehicles to be line-fitted with automatic transmission. From the end of 1998 the North American market also received the new Td5.

Specifications

Land Rover Defender 90 200 Tdi

Engine	2,495cc diesel direct injection four-cylinder
	Bore/stroke: 90.47mm/97mm
	Compression ratio: 19.5:1
Power	107bhp @ 3,800rpm
Torque	288lb/ft @ 1,800rpm
Steering	Recirculating ball with power assistance
Transmission	Five-speed permanent four-wheel drive
	with transfer box and lockable centre diff
Suspension	Front, beam axle with leading arms and
	Panhard rod, coil springs and telescopic
	dampers; rear, beam axle with trailing
	arms, central A-frame, coil springs and
	telescopic dampers
Brakes	Front, 11.8in (300mm) discs; rear, 11in
	(279mm) drums; vacuum servo
Dimensions	Wheelbase 92.9in (2.36m); track 58.5in
	(1.49m); length 146.5in (3.72m); width
	70.5in (1.79m); height 77.6in (1.97m)
	(hardtop); unladen weight 3,734lb
	(1,695kg); max payload 1,556lb (706kg)
Wheels/tyres	16in/205 16 (standard)
Fuel capacity	12gal (54.5l)
Max speed	84mph (135kph)
0–60mph (0–96kph)	17.4sec
Consumption	23–27mpg

Land Rover Defender 90 Td5

Engine	2,492cc diesel direct injection five-cylinder
	Bore/stroke: 84.45mm/88.95mm
	Compression ratio: 19.5:1
Power	122bhp @ 4,200rpm
Torque	195lb/ft @ 1,950rpm
Transmission	Five-speed permanent four-wheel drive
	with transfer box and lockable centre diff;
	electronic traction control optional (with
	ABS)
Wheels/tyres	16in/7.50 R16 (standard)
Fuel capacity	13.2gal (60l)
Max speed	85mph (137kph)
0–60mph (0–96kph)	16sec
Fuel consumption	24–28mpg

Suspension, steering, and dimensions as before, except: unladen weight 3,836lb (1,741kg); max payload 1,350lb (613kg) (hardtop).

The world's best off-roader

There is no other generally available, off-the-shelf, dual-purpose vehicle with the off-roading capabilities of the Land Rover Defender. It is the natural choice for serious off-road competition and the favoured machine for a large proportion of the world's recreational off-roaders. Even in the USA, where there's a tradition of fine, home-grown 4x4s and where the Defender's penetration into the market has been relatively small, 90s figure strongly when groups of enthusiasts take to the hills.

The reputation for being able to cope with extremely rough terrain was established with the very first Land Rovers, which were more capable

The reputation of the Land Rover grew as it progressed from Series I to Series III, with the most important factors being toughness, reliability and off-road ability. The interest in recreational off-roading grew alongside the development of the vehicles, playing an increasing role in the general public's perception of Land Rovers. (Nick Dimbleby)

off the tarmac than the only alternative four-wheel drive vehicle available, the ex-military Willys Jeep. The American vehicle was good, but the Land Rover had the edge.

The Land Rover legend developed with its growing popularity around much of the globe as a working vehicle. Farmers, construction workers, and forestry teams took them everywhere, while adventurous individuals used them for weekend fun and, occasionally, trans-continental expeditions. If you wanted to drive where other road-going machinery couldn't go, you went by Land Rover.

Solihull improved the vehicles constantly as they progressed through Series II, IIA, and III, but it became increasingly apparent from the mid-1970s onwards that two principal aspects would have to be put right if they were to retain their great popularity: the engines were old-fashioned and inadequate, and the leaf spring suspension was too firm and somewhat restricting in off-road situations. The launch of the One Ten in 1983, followed the next year by the Ninety, mostly rectified these shortcomings. Coil springing totally overcame the criticisms relating to the earlier suspension and, as the new series progressed, the engines also became much more suitable.

In the face of growing numbers of increasingly good 4x4s from the USA and the Far East, it was not true to say that Series IIIs stood head and shoulders above the rest when it came to off-

Not very practical on a cold day, but at least everything is easily accessible! (Nick Dimbleby)

roading, as earlier models had; but the original One Ten and Ninety put this right at a stroke. And with better engines, culminating in the 200 Tdi introduced with the adoption of the Defender name, it became ever-more difficult for other vehicles to rival the utility Land Rovers over rough ground. In fact, the only opposition came from, firstly, the Range Rover, and then the Discovery.

Awkwardly for Land Rover, right from its launch in 1970, the Range Rover had been a superior off-roader to the tail-end Series IIA and, from 1971, the Series III. The company promoted the Series III, as it had all previous Land Rovers, as the 'go-anywhere vehicle, unbeatable on farm, track or mountain', yet anyone who had driven a Range Rover off-road knew very well that it would keep going long after a Series III had been brought to a standstill.

The Range Rover was the world's best off-roader – but only until 1983.

The Defender reigns

The development of the new-generation utility Land Rovers was not the most scientific project the automotive world has ever known, and it began much later than it should have done with somewhat less enthusiasm than it might have had. That it resulted in such excellent vehicles, destined

The most significant improvement achieved with the introduction of the Defender family was the dramatic increase in axle articulation resulting from the switch from leaf to coil springs. Axle articulation is the single most-important consideration in an off-roader, followed by engine torque characteristics. (Nick Dimbleby)

Although Land Rover had used leaf springs from the beginning, the limitation they impose on axle articulation meant that none of these vehicles could match the off-road performance of the Ninety and One Ten. (Dave Barker)

to take Land Rover into the 21st century, would be something of a surprise to any present-day motor industry analyst.

Like most 4x4s, the Defender is a compromise. But whereas other all-terrain vehicles are designed principally for road work, usually with compromised off-road ability, Land Rover's

tradition ensured that the original Ninety and One Ten would be, firstly, working off-road utilities, and secondly, road-going light trucks.

The Range Rover had already proved that, despite being principally a road-going estate car, there need be little, if any, compromise in off-roading capability, and the Discovery and second-generation Range Rover have continued the theme. But only the Solihull factory has been able to achieve that fine blend.

It was different with the Defender family, which had to be capable of the same hard work in the same unforgiving conditions as had the earlier Series Land Rovers. You can have a true working vehicle which is acceptable on the road but, as the Japanese had found, it is much more difficult to design a road-going vehicle with high levels of passenger comfort which is also capable of carrying loads of rubble, barrels of oil, or dead sheep.

In many ways, the vehicle which comes closest to the concept of the working Land Rover is the Toyota Hi-Lux 4x4 pick-up truck, but even this, good as it is, is nowhere near as capable in bad

This photograph shows the Defender beam axle very clearly. As well as working brilliantly with the springing, the axle casing itself is enormously strong, and protects the half shafts from accidental damage. (Dave Barker)

R739 CUG

conditions as a Land Rover. And that is perhaps the best illustration of what Land Rover achieved when the One Ten was in the design stage.

Solihull didn't take the easy way out when the Range Rover's chassis, suspension and transmission were used for the One Ten. There was no way of improving on the systems which had been developed in the late-1960s and, as time has proved conclusively, nothing better has emerged since. By marrying these crucial aspects of chassis and suspension design to the type of bodies used for previous generations of utility models, Land Rover was able to come up with a working vehicle which could operate in conditions which would stop anything else. By refusing to compromise on the working nature of the vehicles, Land Rover knew that the One Ten and Ninety and, in time, the Defender, would be less car-like on the road than most other 4x4s.

In making these decisions the people at Solihull were completely correct, as history has proved. And it is because of this resolute approach that the

The use of beam axles in Land Rovers is considered by some to be rather out-of-step with modern automotive thinking. Yet it is precisely this aspect of design, along with the use of long-travel low-rate springs, which gives the Land Rover its advantage over the opposition, where independent suspension rules the day. (Nick Dimbleby)

Defender has become so universally popular with the enthusiast movement. For countless thousands of faithful disciples the Defender, in all its forms, with its square-cut and workmanlike lines, its unrivalled off-road ability, and its instant recognisability, is the world's most important vehicle. The fact that design compromises resulted in it being noisy, thirsty, and comparatively slow has merely added to its appeal.

Off-road strengths

The secret of the Defender lies in the strength of its chassis, its long-travelling coil suspension, the refusal of Land Rover to be tempted away from beam axles, and its permanent four-wheel-drive

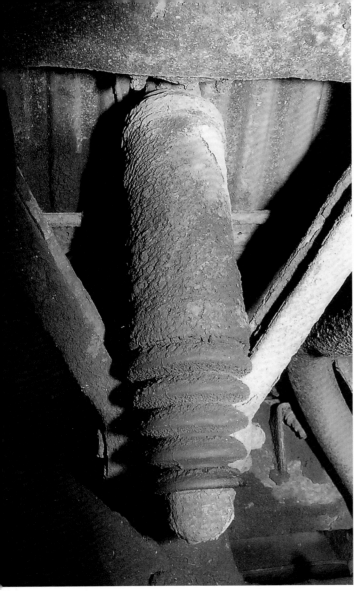

In designing the rear suspension of the One Ten, Land Rover incorporated the Boge self-levelling strut which had been pioneered on the Range Rover with great success. It was offered as standard only on Station Wagons, but many were fitted as options to other versions. (Dave Barker)

transmission. Closely following these features in importance has been a succession of excellent engines: firstly the V8, then the progressively better 200 and 300 Tdi diesels. Of all these characteristics it is the springing and axles which give the Defender its great capability over rough ground. Indeed, only the Range Rover and Discovery, which have near-identical arrangements, are able to compete.

To understand the advantages given by the Defender's suspension, it is necessary first to look

at the drawbacks of other forms of springs and axles. It also helps to appreciate that the single, most important aid to traction when off-roading is to keep all four wheels in firm contact with the surface; the most common cause of becoming immobile, other than when a muddy surface fails to enable the tyre treads to grip, is when one or more wheels lose contact with the surface, or fail to exert sufficient pressure to permit the tyres to transmit enough torque to maintain forward movement.

Anyone with experience of, say, a Series IIA or III Land Rover will be aware of two principal shortcomings when off-roading, both of which are related to the suspension design. Firstly, leaf springs restrict the extent of axle articulation which, in turn, limits the vertical movement of the wheels when encountering holes or upward obstructions; secondly, the way in which the springs are fixed to the underside of the body, by shackle assemblies, forms an obstruction which can easily make such firm contact with the ground that it immobilises the vehicle.

To a lesser or greater degree these factors also apply to many non-Land Rover four-wheel drive vehicles. Most manufacturers stuck resolutely to leaf springs long after Solihull had proved that coil springing was much better for off-roading and, even today, some are still using them. It's a sign, of course, that much of the opposition was not particularly interested in providing exceptional off-road capability in vehicles which, in some cases, were otherwise very good.

By switching to long-travel low-rate (or 'soft') coil springs, Land Rover was able to increase very considerably the axle articulation. With the use of this system in the One Ten Solihull provided 7in (178mm) of wheel travel at the front and 8.25in (210mm) at the rear, an improvement of 50 per cent and 25 per cent respectively over the Series III. The coil springs had the second advantage of greatly reducing the shocks which are inevitable when off-roading, even when doing it correctly and driving very slowly, and improving the on-road ride to a quite remarkable degree.

When Land Rover was developing the Range Rover it resisted the temptation to use independent suspension, either at the front alone or on all four wheels. By sticking to beam axles, which are rigid from end-to-end, and which were used in all the Series vehicles, a further advantage was gained and this was duly carried over into the Defender series.

There are two benefits of solid, beam axles when off-roading. The first is that ground clearance remains more constant beneath the differential than it does with independently sprung axles which, because of their action, can sometimes reduce effective ground clearance. The second, related, advantage is that with beam axles the wheels are less likely to take up the odd angles they adopt over rough ground with independent action. Land Rover tyres therefore mostly have the tread in line with the ground.

By using beam axles in earlier vehicles Land Rover had made the most of its leaf springs, but by retaining them in its new breed of utilities and, at the same time, introducing the long-travel coils which had proved so effective in the Range Rover, the Defender series was given a suspension system which transformed the capabilities of the 'working' vehicles. However, a suspension system of this

In Defenders the small lever used for selecting high or low ratios is also used to lock the centre differential which, by locking the front and rear prop shafts into a 'solid' drive unit, helps to keep the vehicle going when drive is lost on one axle. Locking or limited slip axle differentials are not fitted by Land Rover, but can be added if required. (Nick Dimbleby)

DID YOU KNOW?

Transfer box

The transfer box got its name because, in a 4x4, it provides the mechanism by which power is transferred from the normal gearbox to the prop shafts for the front and rear axles. Its other role of providing a step-down system for low ratios doesn't really have anything to do with its name.

DID YOU KNOW?

Gearing down

It's not a practical proposition to produce a standard gearbox containing all the gear ratios required in an off-roader, and neither would it be practical to use a gearbox with ten or more forward speeds. Apart from the difficulties of using it, such a gearbox would be potentially dangerous if any of the extra-low ratios were selected inadvertently.

type, when used with vehicles which are sometimes very heavily loaded over the roughest terrain imaginable, is subject to extreme forces, sometimes in several directions simultaneously. It is therefore imperative for axle location to be properly and robustly controlled, with a suspension-to-body mounting system capable of taking extreme punishment. Anyone who has stripped-down or replaced sections of a Defender's suspension system will know just how well this has been achieved, and how these vehicles are capable of withstanding the stresses involved in heavy-duty off-roading.

The front axle is located by long, forged steel leading radius arms which prevent the axle from moving forwards and backwards, and a Panhard rod which prevents sideways movement. The radius arms run back from each axle end to the chassis and are bolted in position through bushes which permit the vertical movement of the arms as the wheels move up and down. These arms are particularly strong and provide much of the front-end strength for which the Defender's suspension is renowned.

With just one wheel spinning, a Defender will usually come to a halt if the centre differential has not been locked because of the way all torque transfers to the wheel offering least resistance. Locking the centre differential maintains drive to the other axle and, if both those wheels are gripping, keeps the vehicle on the move. (Dave Barker)

The springs at their lower end are mounted directly to the top of the axle, and are held by particularly tough chassis brackets at the top – a far stronger arrangement than, for example, the MacPherson strut system used on saloon cars, which would not be able to cope with the extreme loadings encountered in off-roading.

Land Rover pioneered an excellent rear suspension arrangement with the Range Rover and this, too, was carried over into the One Ten and Ninety. Fore and aft movement of the axle is firmly located with tubular trailing lower links running from the chassis to the axle, while lateral movement is controlled by an A-frame, which consists of twin upper links running upwards and backwards centrally from the axle and bolted to the chassis on either side. A system of bushes permits full wheel movement.

A further refinement was the fitment on some long-wheelbase models of a Boge self-levelling strut, a self-energising device linking the centre of the axle to the chassis. Effectively, it's a third suspension unit designed to permit full movement of the rear springs when the vehicle is heavily loaded. Unfortunately, however, over the years many owners have neglected to replace worn-out

DID YOU KNOW?

Traction control
The electronic traction control or ETC introduced as an optional extra with the Defender Td5 relies on the ABS system for its operation. If there's a fault with the ABS, you lose ETC as well.

DID YOU KNOW?

Viscous control
Range Rovers have had a viscous-coupled centre differential arrangement for some time, which locks automatically when significant differences in front and rear prop shaft speeds are sensed. However, this has not been included in the specification of the Defender Td5 series because it was felt the more arduous working conditions would require manual rather than automatic operation.

self-levellers, with the result that load-carrying 110s can be inhibited off-road because of restricted spring movement. With the unit operating correctly even an overloaded vehicle retains most, if not all, of its axle articulation.

The Defender's transmission also has a lot to do with its off-road capability. Because it is a permanent four-wheel drive system, there isn't the need to manually select 4x4 when the going gets tough, as is the case with most rival vehicles. Torque from the engine is delivered via the main gearbox to a transfer gearbox, which provides the choice of high or low range, and from there to front and rear propeller shafts. A centre differential within the transfer gearbox permits different rotation speeds between the two prop shafts, thereby preventing the build-up of stresses in the transmission (transmission wind-up) which would otherwise be inevitable when cornering because of the smaller turning radius taken by the rear axle. Each axle has conventional differentials.

The centre diff, another aspect of the Defender range first used in the Range Rover, can be locked by moving the secondary gear lever (used for selecting high or low ratios) over to the left. When this is done the front and rear prop shafts are effectively locked together. Without this facility, simply losing grip with one wheel would bring a Defender to a standstill. This happens because whenever a wheel loses traction all the torque for that axle takes the line of least resistance and moves to the spinning wheel; the other wheel is simply starved of power. Without a centre diff, or with the unit in its 'free' position, all torque from the gearbox would go to the prop shaft feeding the axle with the spinning wheel, leaving the other axle

Extreme caution must be exercised when driving in water without a high-level air intake. The slightest amount of water entering the inlet system can damage an engine very seriously; diesels are best for wading because of the lack of an electrical ignition system. (Nick Dimbleby)

without power. By locking the centre diff the loss of traction to just one wheel only deprives that axle of driving ability. Because the two prop shafts are locked, they both continue to turn at the same speed and, provided both wheels on the second axle are gripping, the vehicle will continue to move. However, if traction is lost by one wheel on each axle, the vehicle will stop, regardless of the centre diff. This can only be overcome by the fitment of locking, or limited slip, diffs to replace the standard axle units (see Chapter 11).

Engines for off-roading

As well as the Defender's excellent suspension and transmission, the third factor which greatly affects its off-road performance is the engine and, more specifically, its torque characteristics and whether it is petrol or diesel.

Outright brake horse power is of little advantage when off-roading, although clearly it makes a difference to main road performance. Rather, it is torque which is required for off-roading and for heavy-duty towing work, and the lower the revs

needed to produce maximum torque the more it can be made to work for you.

A further point regarding engines concerns the difference between petrol and diesel when it comes to off-road reliability and performance. Initially, the One Ten came with either 2.25-litre petrol and diesel engines, both low on power and torque, or the tried and tested 3.5-litre petrol V8. The Ninety came without a V8 option to start with, having the good old 2.25-litre petrol and the newly enlarged 2.5-litre diesel. The 2.5 diesel was a little better than the one it replaced, but not much, although it wasn't a bad off-road unit.

The V8 had proved itself an excellent off-road engine in the Range Rover, and in the early days of the Defender family was the preferred option for enthusiasts. At the time it was introduced for

With the centre diff lock engaged, a Land Rover will cross with ease the sort of ditches which will almost certainly stop other types of vehicle not possessing the axle articulation of the Defender. Ditches must never be tackled head-on. (Nick Dimbleby)

the Ninety, in 1985, it produced 114bhp; more importantly, its torque figure was 185lb/ft at 2,500rpm. For off-roading you need to get your torque at a slower engine speed than this, but even at 2,000rpm the torque was better than the opposition could manage. The drawback of the V8, as with all petrol engines, has always been the great difficulty of waterproofing the electrical system sufficiently to prevent misfires or complete stoppage when there's deep water about. A diesel will run completely submerged, provided there's a high-level air intake. Not so a petrol unit.

The introduction of the 2.5-litre Diesel Turbo in late 1986 at last gave the One Ten and Ninety the right engine to match the rest of their off-road superiority. It was not as good as the Tdi would prove to be a few years later, but with this engine the Land Rovers had the combination of diesel dependability for off-road work, and decent power and torque figures. It's worth taking a look at the figures for Land Rover and its competitors at the time the Diesel Turbo took over from the normally-

On a muddy hill climb like this the excellent torque characteristics of the Tdi engine give the best chance of getting to the top. Engines which produce their maximum torque at a higher engine speed are unable to produce the smooth and controllable power flow needed in these situations. (Nick Dimbleby)

aspirated engine, and to compare all these with the 200 Tdi.

	Power	Torque
	(bhp/rpm)	(lb/ft/rpm)
Land Rover 3.5 V8	114 @ 4,000	185 @ 2,500
Land Rover 2.5 D	67 @ 4,000	114 @ 1,800
Land Rover 2.5 DT	85 @ 4,000	150 @ 1,800
Daihatsu Fourtrak 2.8 TD	87 @ 3,600	155 @ 2,200
Isuzu Trooper 2.2 TD	74 @ 4,000	125 @ 2,500
Mercedes 300 3.0 GD	80 @ 4,000	126 @ 2,400
Mitsubishi Shogun 2.4 TD	84 @ 4,200	148 @ 2,000
Nissan Patrol 3.2 D	95 @ 3,600	160 @ 1,800
Toyota Landcruiser 4.0 D	99 @ 3,500	171 @ 1,800
From 1990		
Land Rover 2.5 Tdi	107 @ 3,800	188 @ 1,800

This clearly shows the massive strides made by Land Rover in the progression from its first turbocharged engine to, eventually, the Tdi. Examination of the torque figures highlights the difference between

Anyone expecting to indulge in serious off-roading should fit a winch, and learn how to use it effectively and safely. Off-road trips are less of a worry if there is a winch available to haul you out, should you get stuck, so fitting one makes sense even if you do not usually do more than a spot of greenlaning. (Nick Dimbleby)

Land Rover, from the 2.5 DT onwards, and most of the competition. Only the Shogun's excellent engine, and the huge Toyota, have similar torque characteristics, but even these are sidelined from 1990 onwards with the appearance in the Defender of the Tdi. And it is worth noting the Tdi's torque superiority over even the Rover V8.

Driving experience

Only by driving different vehicles off-road can you appreciate the superiority of the Defender. During the mid-1980s my own V8 One Ten County Station Wagon, one of the earliest, was used as everyday transport and for off-road fun. At the same time my work enabled me to gain considerable off-roading experience in Mitsubishi Shoguns, Daihatsu Fourtraks, a Mercedes G-Wagen, and an Isuzu Trooper. The experience was most illuminating and gave me an early, yet permanent, appreciation of the superiority of the Defender series.

As has been explained, the Land Rover gains its principal advantage from its suspension and beam axle arrangement, but in practice it's the way everything performs which makes the difference. Take a simple and frequently encountered obstacle, such as a ditch crossing. Unless the surrounding terrain makes it impossible, a ditch should always be crossed diagonally, so that only one wheel risks being out of contact with the surface at a time as it drops into the depression. The long travel of a Land Rover's coil springs with the associated extreme axle articulation means that a Defender will frequently cross such an obstacle with ease. With the centre diff lock engaged you stand a good chance of 'walking' the vehicle through in first gear

The most spectacular form of vehicle recovery is the kinetic energy (or KERR) method, whereby a stretchable rope between the stuck and recovery Land Rover is coiled on the ground before the recovery vehicle takes off at high speed, literally plucking the immobile machine from its mud trap. (Dave Barker)

DID YOU KNOW?

Auto choice

Although automatic transmission is frowned upon by many British off-road enthusiasts, it has distinct advantages in many difficult situations. On slippery climbs and in deep mud you are less likely to lose traction with an auto than with manual gears. Some Defenders have been converted to automatic, and the 50th anniversary limited edition Defender was supplied with V8 engine and auto box as standard. If you're offered one, don't turn it down automatically.

DID YOU KNOW?

Deep water

Without deep wading equipment a Land Rover should not be driven through water which reaches higher than the upper point of the wheel rim. Any deeper and you risk drawing water into the air intake and then into the engine, when serious damage is inevitable. With a high-level air intake and raised breathers for the gearboxes, etc, a diesel Land Rover will run quite happily with water lapping over the bonnet. It ruins the seats and carpets, though!

low ratios and the diesel engine running at tickover … even if there's a ridge on one side of the ditch, or the sides of the obstacle are particularly uneven, very muddy, or both.

But it is far less easy with a vehicle fitted with leaf springs, or with short-travel coils and, probably, independent front suspension. The suspension may cause the front diff to dig in with one wheel pushed up as far as it will go and the other dangling uselessly on the end of its spring.

Climbing awkward, tight, rocky sections is another example where a lack of axle articulation, reduced ground clearance because of independent suspension, and poor throttle response at low revs will stop you. But a Land Rover diesel, especially a

Tdi, will take it with ease, climbing with no or very little throttle input (in first low) as the tyres resolutely clamber over each rock. If you need some power for a particularly steep section, it comes immediately you apply just a touch more throttle, and you remain fully in control.

If hampered by less pliant independent suspension and, again, with ground clearance possibly being reduced by vertical movement of the wheels, it's far less straightforward. Furthermore, if the engine doesn't produce sufficient torque unless it's turning at 2,000rpm or more – and this is very often the case – you're obliged to tackle the section with quite a bit of throttle, and consequently, more speed than you'd like.

Muddy hill climbs can be very difficult, whatever vehicle you're driving, but the torque of the Land Rover Tdi engine gives you the best chance of success in many situations. For example, if it's dangerous to attempt the climb quickly – speed is sometimes the best answer with mud – the only solution is to tackle it at modest speed, but in a relatively high gear, such as third or even fourth

(low ratios). The Tdi will cope with this because it produces lots of torque without requiring a heavy right foot. Many other engines, though, will not let you do this and will simply stall.

Experts and expeditions

Being built on an enormously strong chassis gives the Land Rover a huge advantage over other off-roaders. The chassis imbues massive strength to the entire structure, it reduces under-body vulnerability, it gives uniquely strong mounting points for the suspension, and it facilitates the addition of winches and recovery points with ruggedness impossible in monocoque structures.

Heavy duty winches are essential for extreme off-roading, and for much expedition work. To fit one to a Land Rover Defender you can, if you wish, bolt

What the well-equipped expedition vehicle is wearing. Thorough vehicle preparation is essential before any trip to the Sahara, Middle East, or further, and items such as a full expedition roof rack, under-body protection, water and fuel containers are essential. (Nick Dimbleby)

it directly to the front bumper, a solid steel affair which is, in turn, bolted to the main chassis frame. Consequently a winch recovery with a Land Rover passes the stresses through the chassis without any of it affecting the body. It is, in fact, possible to suspend a Defender on a suitably strong cable without any risk of damage – television advertising some years ago which showed a Defender being winched up a near-vertical dam retaining wall at a Welsh reservoir involved no trickery, just some unseen safety measures.

The most dramatic way to recover a stranded vehicle from impossibly deep mud, or a bog, is to use the kinetic energy recovery system. This involves a stretchable but very strong rope being attached to the front of the stranded vehicle and to the rear of the one doing the recovery, which is positioned with its rear just a few feet from the one which is stuck. The rope is loosely coiled between the two, the recovery vehicle takes off as rapidly as possible, and the energy stored within the tightly stretched rope yanks the stuck Land Rover clear.

It's all very dramatic, and not a little dangerous, but would be impossible with vehicles not possessing the chassis strength of the Land Rover. To do this, the recovery rope must be attached to a strong point on the front of the first Land Rover, which is usually a pair of recovery attachments known as JATE rings, first developed for military use. These are bolted to the main chassis legs and the incredible stresses involved pass through the attachments and into the chassis. Usually, the rope will be attached to the recovery Land Rover's towball or pintle, although this can only be done when the towball is in line with the forces involved, and the tow bar is properly attached to the rear crossmember. Provided there's no deep rust on the crossmember or rear chassis the vehicle has no problem with the forces involved.

It's because of its chassis, and the way the towing equipment is connected directly to it, that a Land Rover can tow incredibly heavy loads. Naturally, there are strict laws governing towing in normal circumstances, but it is not unusual for Defenders to be called on to tow fully loaded heavy trucks for short distances. Police patrols do it regularly with Defenders, Range Rovers, and

A clear illustration of the lack of structural strength in the upper bodywork of Land Rovers. (Nick Dimbley)

Discoverys when broken-down HGVs need moving urgently. For more normal towing work with caravans and horseboxes Defenders are ideal. The torque of the Tdi or V8 engine copes easily with this sort of work, while the size, weight, and design of the vehicles makes them just about the best tow cars imaginable.

For more adventurous travelling, such as long-haul overland trips through Third World territories, Land Rovers have been the way to go since the birth of the marque in 1948. The Defender 110 Tdi is the perfect expedition vehicle, offering excellent mechanical reliability, long range, spacious accommodation, and almost unrivalled load-carrying capability. These factors, along with the Defender's all-terrain prowess and, with an expedition-style roof rack, more than ample space for a roof-top tent, make it the preferred choice for a high proportion of long-distance trekkers.

Chapter **Seven**

Testing times

Motoring journalists have been supportive of Land Rover since its earliest days, when they wrote with undisguised enthusiasm about the very first model. Solihull's first all-new vehicle since those times, the Range Rover, was also greeted with massive praise, which has continued to the present day. And so, too, has been the Defender, which, although falling beyond the everyday remit of most car publications, has received wide coverage in Station Wagon form in all the mainstream motoring magazines. Almost without exception the comments have been favourable, even when written by journalists who didn't fully understand the vehicle, as has sometimes been the case.

Land Rover has always understood the importance of first-hand road tests of its vehicles. Going back to 1948, it made early production models available to journalists, and this has been the company's policy ever since.

Although part of Rover, then British Leyland, then Rover Group, then BMW, and finally Ford, Land Rover itself has always been a small company when compared with mainstream manufacturers and, consequently, has never been able to justify a large fleet of press vehicles. But it has always done its best to make test vehicles available to newspapers, magazines, and television shows. Positive press comment is the best form of promotion a car maker can have, and it speaks volumes for the confidence within Land Rover that vehicles have been made available to such a wide variety of media outlets. It's reassuring, too, that in recent years Solihull has loaned Defenders to the

enthusiast press, knowing very well that the vehicle is setting out to take part in an off-road event in France, for example, with a high chance of bodywork damage.

Yet it's the mainstream motoring press, read by knowledgeable motorists and by potential buyers in search of unbiased information, that has always been the most meaningful for Land Rover. Here's what writers around the world have said about the Defender series, from pre-Defender days to the Tdi.

Launch week

In the week of March 1983 when the new coil-sprung Land Rover was launched, *Autocar* carried a fully descriptive article packed with detail. The magazine clearly recognised the great importance of the One Ten and went to great lengths to make sure its readers fully understood the technical background. There wasn't a great deal of editorial comment to be found amid the factual information, but what there was showed considerable under-standing and not a little foresight:

‘The concept of the One Ten is to combine the traditional ruggedness, reliability and longevity of the Land Rover with the better riding, better handling, more sophisticated suspension system of the Range Rover. Land Rovers have been around since 1948, Range Rovers since 1970; the One Ten is long overdue.

Its introduction could not have been delayed much longer. The demand for four-wheel drive vehicles in the developing world is still strong, and more and more manufacturers are muscling in on the 4x4 market with vehicles that have as good or better off-road capability than the traditional Land Rover yet offer more car-like, more comfortable passenger accommodation. While Land Rover Ltd's own Range Rover still offers probably the best compromise of on-road refinement and off-road ability, it is expensive, particularly when compared with its adequately competent competition, notably that offered by the Japanese.

Land Rover have shied away from making the One Ten too car-like. It is still very much a utility machine, and Land Rover want it to look that way. Hence passenger accommodation is little changed, and the cab remains functional, retaining such primitive features as sliding windows, and under-screen flap fresh air ventilation.

Functional it may be, but there can be no doubt that the One Ten is a vast improvement, boosting Land Rover's competitiveness in an increasingly hard-fought sector of the market. The improvement in on-road ride alone should be enough to regain the loyalty of many who might have been tempted to buy foreign in the search for a reasonably priced utility with reasonable levels of refinement. The One Ten also has considerably better off-road capability.'

Specialist view

The first reference to the new One Ten in a specialist magazine came in the May 1983 issue of *Overlander*, then Britain's only off-road publication. Again, as befits the importance of the vehicle, the write-up was largely technical, but there were some observations as well, Brian Hartley's closing comment being particular prophetic:

'The One Ten can only be really appreciated from the driving seat. It is there that all regular and seasoned Land Rover, and for that matter, Range Rover drivers had better prepare for a severe case of culture shock.

The One Ten's on- and off-road driving manners came as something of a revelation to one who was weaned on the 'old' type Land Rovers (the One Ten having aged the original vehicle at a stroke). Taken as a whole the driving experience was more impressive than either the Range Rover or the Mercedes G-Wagen. The latter vehicle in particular is going to have a hard time against the One Ten in every aspect except the passenger compartment.

It would require far harsher conditions than those we encountered to really test the mettle of the One Ten, but I

From the very earliest days of the One Ten and Ninety, motoring journalists were writing enthusiastically about the capabilities of the new vehicles. (Nick Dimbleby)

would happily put money on its coil sprung rump to match any of the competition, from whatever continent, in an all-out off-road test, including its own stable mates.

Could it be, I wonder, that we are witnessing the birth of a new legend? **'**

V8 Pick-Up

The same writer was at it again in January 1984. This time *Overlander* was doing a full test on a One Ten V8 High-Capacity Pick-Up, and a little bit of aggravation became mixed with a lot of praise:

'The cab leaked a lot. The passenger side had two distinct leaks, one from behind the plush pressed felt headlining and the other from behind the dash scuttle. From other sources I believe this is not an isolated case and does not bode well for the long-term future of the trim in particular.

Off-road the One Ten behaved exactly as you would expect a vehicle with its breeding. Laden or unladen it took everything in its stride. Ditches and sharp hummocks, which are

usually the real stoppers for leaf-sprung vehicles, were taken with ease, keeping the driver and, just as important, the load on an even keel. It also allowed any such obstacles to be taken gently, rather than 'with a run', again resulting in a softer ride for whatever or whoever was being carried.

At 14mpg the consumption was better than I had expected as the vehicle had been used hard for stop/start runs, off-road testing and full loads. The 4-cylinder versions would probably be better on fuel consumption, but with those sort of payloads the lack of power would be painfully evident.

One thing is certain, in its class the V8 One Ten HCPU has no competitor in terms of off-road performance. **'**

Early adventures

Two of the earliest off-roading stories involving the new vehicles were those in *Autocar* in March 1983, detailing a journey to Scotland which was made before the launch of the One Ten, and an excellent feature in the rival weekly *Motor* in September the

following year, in which the new Ninety was put through its paces.

Autocar's article was, in fact, part of a feature introducing the One Ten, in which the journalists managed to get the vehicle bogged down within feet of starting their drive along a track in Skye, and hopelessly cross-axled on General Wade's military road in the Western Highlands when reversing. Nonetheless, the article was in general extremely complimentary, although it did include a comment about finding a limit to the One Ten's ability which, although true, should have been accompanied by an admission of the journalists' own recklessness in failing to take due care where they took the vehicle. Competent off-road drivers would not have got stuck where *Autocar* did.

The feature by *Motor* on the Ninety was

altogether different. It was written by freelance Phil Llewellyn, who does know what he's doing, and involved driving a 2,286cc petrol-engined Ninety for several days along very challenging ancient tracks in some of the remotest parts of Wales. Sensibly, Llewellyn and photographer Tim Wren were accompanied by a winch-equipped One Ten.

In an excellently written and stimulating feature the capabilities of the Ninety and One Ten were thoroughly endorsed after driving through some of the most difficult green lanes anywhere – one seven-mile (11km) stretch took seven hours, which is a good measure of the sort of test the Ninety was put to. There was plenty of winching, but the magazine didn't contain a single note of criticism about either of the two vehicles, both of which had proved much better than expected. Unlike some other journalists who drove the new Land Rovers with the old four-cylinder petrol engine, Llewellyn accepted the lack of power as a characteristic of the unit and drove accordingly, both on- and off-road. It would be interesting to know by how much more he'd have enjoyed it with a V8 or, looking to the future, a Tdi.

The Defender has always had considerable appeal as an everyday vehicle. Its excellent road-going performance went down very well with *Autocar* when it tested a V8 in 1985. (Nick Dimbleby)

V8 Ninety

The lack of a V8 option for the Ninety on its introduction was the source of considerable dissatisfaction, but when the big petrol engine did come along in the short-wheelbase model it was greeted with great joy. Among the magazines covering the extension of the V8 option, plus five-speed gearbox, into the Ninety was *Autocar*, with a short but enthusiastic piece published on 8 May 1985:

❛The short wheelbase Land Rover is now available with 3.5-litre V8 engine and five-speed gearbox, giving vastly improved on-road performance and refinement and exhilarating off-road ability.

The big change is under the bonnet. Twitch the engine into life and there is a satisfying burble from the big exhaust pipe. Twin Zenith Stromberg 175 CDSE carbs hiss gently beneath the cylinder banks. Engage first, step on the pedal and – by Land Rover standards anyway – the car rockets forwards. The most impressive feature is that on a long run it is quite easy to get 90mph up on the speedometer, and to cruise at 85mph on part throttle.

Off-road the V8 Ninety must now rival the Range Rover as the Best Off-road car in the World. Permanent 4wd with central differential lock, all round long travel coil spring suspension follows the Range Rover pattern, and the short wheelbase and steeper angles of approach and departure mean even better ability on tortuous terrain.

It's not all good news. Big power in a chunky car means a thirst for fuel. We measured consumption at 13.2mpg, though, in fairness to the car, we drove it hard during its short stay with us – fast on the motorway or in low ratio on the rough. A less exuberant owner should get around 15mpg, and 17mpg could be available to someone with particularly light feet.'

Enter the turbo

Before the Tdi there was the Diesel Turbo. In March 1987, soon after the turbocharged 2.5-litre diesel had been introduced, *Autocar* carried out a full

Even before the advent of the Tdi, the County Station Wagon was a force to be reckoned with. *Autocar* **was very impressed with a Diesel Turbo version tested in 1987. (Nick Dimbleby)**

road test on a Ninety County Station Wagon fitted with the new engine:

'When turbocharging the 2.5-litre diesel, Land Rover's engineers were not concerned with outright performance – rather they wanted an engine with plenty of low and mid-range pulling power and no significant turbo lag. With a peak output of 85bhp at 4,000rpm though, the Land Rover has more power than the Mitsubishi Shogun and Isuzu Trooper turbo diesels, and only 2bhp less than Daihatsu's 2.7-litre unit. It also produces a good deal more torque than most of its competitors and, at 1,800rpm, peak torque occurs lower down the rev band.

The end result is an engine that has a remarkable ability to pull from low rpm with no discernible turbo lag in normal use. Hence the Ninety feels quite rapid on the road with a broad spread of power.

Power doesn't come for free, and the turbo diesel's extra horses have taken their toll on the fuel consumption. An overall figure of 18mpg doesn't sound impressive at first, and indeed it is bettered by several of the Land Rover's Japanese

Whether it is a caravan, horsebox or conventional trailer, Defenders are excellent towing vehicles. (Nick Dimbleby)

competitors. The figure does reflect the hard time the Land Rover was given during its time with us ... the average owner could certainly expect to attain 20mpg.

Off-road ability is still at the heart of the success of the Land Rover range, in contrast to some of its competitors where highway comfort is the main attraction. The Ninety turbo diesel does not disappoint in that respect and is surpassed in off-road ability only by V8-engined versions. The car seems almost unstoppable, and once a gear has been selected to tackle an obstacle the driver can concentrate on the task of selecting the right line.

The Ninety is a superb off-roader that is equally at home on the road, with good handling and an excellent ride. In County guise it offers virtually the same equipment levels as its Japanese rivals and at £12,783 it is priced competitively with them. If conversation is not high on the list of priorities it would make an excellent motorway cruiser for a large family.

For a long time in the '70s, Land Rover traded on its reputation and little else. The steady stream of improvements started with the One Ten have brought it bang up to date though, and with the latest Ninety the company has demonstrated you no longer need to be merely a patriot to buy a Land Rover.'

The first Tdi

Although a very worthwhile improvement, the first turbocharged engine was not in the same league as the second, the all-new 200 Tdi. This entered service with the Discovery in 1989, then went to the utility production line the following year, transforming what were now known as the Defender 90, 110, and 130. One of the early Defender Tdi write-ups was in *Car*. What did this no-nonsense, hard-hitting publication have to say?

'Apart from the grille name badges and nasty Defender door decals, what is new is the switch to the excellent direct injection 2.5-litre Tdi diesel introduced on the Discovery.

In its first year the 200 Tdi has proved remarkably reliable and engineers claim it matches the specific fuel consumption of the best truck diesels.

The horsebox frequently hitched to the back of a Discovery isn't lightweight, but Land Rovers traditionally work harder for their living, drivers revving them for long periods in low gears.

For this reason the peak has been taken off the power curve, leaving the Land Rover on 107bhp at 3,800rpm, compared with the Discovery's 111bhp at 4,000rpm. Torque is now 188lb/ft at 1,800rpm, instead of 195lb/ft for the sister vehicle.

Stand next to the Tdi at idle and it barely registers as an oil-burner, so suppressed is the diesel 'knock'. But the most convincing improvement comes when the Land Rover 110 County is faced with a long incline, something which would have had its predecessor wheezing and dawdling. The new engine neither struggles nor kicks up a din.

Off-road it would take a full load to dampen the Tdi's remarkable eagerness. Even climbing the steepest inclines the engine feels strong and lusty, not simply dependable. Downhill braking in bottom gear is infinitely reassuring. The workhorse's worthy new lease of life has not come too soon. **'**

Digging deep

While *Car's* readers were noting these comments, the enthusiasts who had bought the latest issue of *Land Rover Owner* were reading a slightly deeper analysis of the Defender Tdi, this time a 90:

'It was easy with Discovery to be dazzled by the new body on the Range Rover chassis and the strikingly roomy and well-designed interior and not spend enough time looking under the bonnet. Yet it was there, as users will by now have found out, that was perhaps the most impressive part of the whole launch package – the 2.5-litre, turbo charged, intercooled, direct injection diesel, designated 200 Tdi.

For the first time, a diesel-engined Land Rover, yielding affordable economy, can easily keep up with – and even be ahead of – other car traffic and find itself in the fast lane of an autoroute at an easy and comfortable 75mph cruise.

As with Discovery, revs and a lot of gear changing are not essential. The extraordinary torque of the Tdi makes fifth gear a useable gear rather than a gear you get into only after accelerating to the speed you want in fourth.

The power steering of the Defender is admirably suited to its role, both in lightness and gearing. Of the two, the gearing and 'speed' of the steering was the more valued attribute.

The suppleness of the Range Rover-type all-coil suspension was soon proven when I took it off-road. Even this suspension, however, will eventually run out of movement and when it did the centre diff lock got me out of trouble – but only just. Land Rover still do not offer an across-the-axle differential lock, so it was possible in extreme situations to get diagonal wheels spinning while the vehicle was suspended on the

wheels at the other two corners.

With the Defender the Land Rover utility models have quietly stepped into a new era of their long career and the steady evolution is apparent throughout the machine. The advent of the Tdi diesel – that actually has fractionally more torque than the V8 – is a milestone for the whole Land Rover range. **'**

Export drives

Throughout its history Land Rover has depended on overseas sales for a sizeable proportion of its income. Australia has always been a good market for Solihull's products, so what did the Australian press, renowned for being outspoken, make of the switch from leaf springs to coil-sprung utilities?

The interior of the 90 Tdi impressed *Land Rover Owner*, **while the Tdi engine was described as a 'milestone' for the entire Land Rover range. (Nick Dimbleby)**

Here are some of the comments made by *Motor Manual* magazine in February 1985:

'The Land Rover as we have come to know it, is dead. In its place is the all-new 110, which is really a Range Rover that looks like a Land Rover.

Despite a number of changes, and continuing refinement, the Landie gradually gave way to the Japanese product swamping the world market. The time came when old ideas had to be replaced by newer ones.

The County Wagon is, of course, to be the main focus of JRA's (Australian importer) Land Rover efforts. A new one million dollar assembly facility at Moorebank in NSW will build all the 110s with the exception of the petrol County which will be initially imported.

The alloy V8 won't be the only power plant available in the County, as the Isuzu 3.8-litre diesel used in previous Land Rovers is listed as an option. Turbocharging for the 3.8 is a predictable extension soon.

Off-road the 110 feels like a Range Rover, yet it doesn't. The long wheelbase adds something to the ride quality that is balanced out by the fact that the springs, while retaining long-travel characteristics, are slightly firmer.

Steep, rutted climbs are more comfortable in a 110 than most because you've got that long-reaching suspension keeping all four wheels in contact with the ground.

The 110 is as comfortable and secure a way of going off-roading as anything else we know. It's a top-class bush track cruiser that will both get you there safely, and leave you relatively refreshed at the end of the day.

The new Land Rover is very competitive with the Japanese in value for money – and way ahead for all-round ability. Long live the British!'

Problems, problems

One of Land Rover's traditional weaknesses has been poor build quality, and the Defender series has been affected just as much by this as any other Solihull vehicle. The journalist who tested a One Ten for the Australian *4x4* magazine in July 1985 had plenty to complain about:

'During the test the ash tray self destructed and the dashboard as a whole had more rattles than a millionaire's baby. One door wouldn't lock at all, the passenger side front door would not open from the outside and the driver's door would not open from the inside.

The dust sealing around the rear door was abysmal, and the exterior mirror mounts were too flexible – the mirrors vibrated, and made it almost impossible to get a clear picture of what was coming up behind.

I'm told that the clunks and thuds from the transmission are built in to both the 110 and the Range Rover. They also have the same ultra slow gear change problem. There's no such thing as a snap change.

Travelling at any speed above 60kph with both the front windows down produces wind buffeting of a high order. In fact, it's impossible to keep a peaked cap on one's head unless you do the straps up to a point that would do justice to a well applied tourniquet.'

However:

'The 110 took everything in its stride ... Regardless of the conditions the ride was, to say the least, comfortable ... The V8 engine was superb, delivering smooth power throughout the range ... The quietness of the motor is a big plus for the 110 ... The Landy 110 is surprisingly nimble off-road despite its size.

Apart from a little mishap in deep ruts, the 110 felt invincible. Hot but invincible. There seems to be an excessive amount of exhaust heat transferred through the floor, and driving in bare feet was almost out of the question.'

Out of Africa

South Africa was also important to Solihull, and in March 1990 *Car South Africa* reported on a test involving a V8 One Ten County Station Wagon. Included among the comments, which were generally favourable, was a much-heard cry for axle diff locks as well as the built-in lockable centre diff. Unfortunately, local taxation makes Land Rovers costly in South Africa.

'The rich-on-character V8 provides the One Ten Station Wagon with enough urge to go with the latest semi-civilised body treatment. The test model was fitted with the 'Hiline' trim, which includes an oddments bin between the front seats, metallic paint, air conditioning and power steering, cord cloth

The Australian publication *Motor Manual*, wrote with great enthusiasm about the new range of coil-sprung Land Rovers, describing them as 'top class bush track cruisers'. (Nick Dimbleby)

upholstery, carpeting and radio/tape combo.

Of course the Land Rover earned its reputation off-road and this is where the vehicle is most at home. Its strongest feature is an enormous amount of ground clearance, thanks to beam axles front and rear, which does away with the necessity for the suspension links used on independent set-ups that can snag on ruts, boulders and other obstructions.

After venturing into slippery marsh we concluded that we would have preferred a diff lock on each of the axles as well as the centre diff lock, because when both front and rear sets of wheels are on slippery ground power tends to spin out of a wheel on each axle, leaving the vehicle bogged down.

This does not happen in most situations that the Land Rover is likely to encounter, because of the supple suspension. In mud and over mounds its capability is truly excellent.

The fact that the vehicle relies heavily on imported parts, despite being produced at Leyland's Blackheath plant, pushes the price up to R104,390, which is a tough one to swallow. But if you are serious about travelling off-road, this one had better be on your shopping list. **'**

Spicy sport

Until 1982, the Camel Trophy used Range Rovers for the annual combination exercise of impossible driving conditions, bridge building, and other tasks in remote parts of the tropics, switching to Series IIIs for 1983. Then, to publicise and celebrate the new Land Rover, One Tens were used for the fifth anniversary event in Brazil. One of the few British magazines to report on the Trophy was *4-Wheel Drive* in its December 1984 issue:

'Diesel engines were chosen for the 20-vehicle strong convoy – fuel economy, low down torque and the ever present danger of fire made this the only choice. The units were the now superseded 2.3-litre engines.

Finally, incredibly, everybody got through and the Trophy was finished. Damage to people? Remarkably, none. Damage to vehicles? Considerable. All of them sustained incredible wounds.

It goes without saying that there is hardly a straight body panel between them, but other maladies include bent chassis, bumpers split like sardine cans and a range of other parts ripped or broken off. But they kept going. **'**

Land Rovers have been used as workhorses in Africa since the earliest days. *Car South Africa* considered the Defender series well worth considering for off-road work in the hostile environment of southern Africa. (Nick Dimbleby)

90 for the USA

Our final word comes from that great American institution *Car and Driver*, which wrote about the first US-certified (or North American Specification) 90 in its February 1994 issue. Land Rover North America had invited the press to the wilds of Wyoming for a taster:

'The Brits at Land Rover in the motherland thought their American pals were off their nut when they asked for a US-certified version of the rugged little Defender 90.

But those boys at Lanham, Maryland, at Land Rover North America know their off-road play toys. Didn't the 500 Defender 110s they brought in a year ago sell instantly? There was no question. They wanted the 92.9-inch wheelbase Tonka truck of dirt diggers in their stateside stable.

The cabin is Spartan; the knobs and the door handles are industrial-looking. The Brits were loathe to use US rubber but are so impressed by these [BF Goodrich Mud Terrains].

Four-wheel disc brakes and four-wheel coil-spring

Defenders were used as support vehicles for the Camel Trophy for many years, where they performed superbly. One Tens were used as competitors' vehicles in the world's toughest driving challenge for the first time in 1984. (Nick Dimbleby)

suspension are the kind of equipment we have come to expect from Land Rover, the kind that sets it apart from the competition. The long-travel coils provide exceptional articulation in rugged terrain; it's really neat to watch a Defender 90 from the rear as it climbs a rocky hill with its front and rear wheels angling in different directions.

The Defender 90 never backed down from anything thrown in its path — from mud to boulders to deep snow that had drifted across our route and marooned a couple of bigger vehicles.

The best option you can choose [if you decide to buy] is an off-road vehicle permit, because not to take this brilliant brute off-road would be a tragedy. It would be like getting your most coveted toy for Christmas and never taking it out of the package.'

Choosing and buying

Choosing

First thoughts

Buying a Land Rover is not like investing in any other vehicle. As ever, a key consideration is cash, often clashing with the desire to buy the best available; but the sheer diversity of the range and width of the age span can make it difficult to get down to a shortlist.

Then there's the question of condition. With Land Rovers the youngest, or lowest-mileage, example in a line-up of price-stickered used vehicles is not necessarily the one in best condition. Unlike conventional cars, which in normal use can be difficult to abuse unduly these days, Land Rovers are subjected to a huge variety of working environments and this impacts severely on their overall condition.

Therefore it is wise never to accept a Land Rover at face value. Those dealer displays of late-model Defenders, gleaming in the sunshine, with immaculate interiors and freshly-blacked tyres, will inevitably contain some which have hardly drawn breath, a couple which have slogged away in front of too-heavy trailers, and perhaps one which went straight from the new-car showroom to chassis-deep, abrasive mud on a motorway construction site.

Simply looking at them, maybe taking a brief test drive in one or two and perhaps glancing over the registration documents, probably will not tell you the engine is prematurely worn, the chassis already rusting or the transmission heading for early failure. This is possible, remember, even with Defenders which are only two or three years old and carrying large price tags, and gives a good idea of the minefield lurking at the other end of the age scale where the prices – and therefore the vehicles – are consequently more attractive to the financially hard-pressed.

Bear that warning in mind, but don't let it deter you if you've never taken the plunge with a Land Rover before, or perhaps if you're trying to move up the scale in terms of age and condition. There are lots of excellent Land Rovers to be had and enjoyed, and while real bargains are few and far between, it is possible – with a combination of homework, perseverance, and shrewd assessment – to end up with the vehicle of your choice without subsequent regrets or nasty letters from your bank.

Key choices

While long-serving Land Rover enthusiasts often know exactly what they want, this is not always the case. Newcomers may have no fixed ideas, or might simply be on the look-out for anything within the Defender family, probably controlled and constrained by a very tight budget, and perhaps ready to buy the first one which comes along at the right price.

However, only the unwise blunder in without first narrowing the choice. There is such a wealth of different types that it is well worth simplifying it by, in the first instance, making a decision regarding the basic type of vehicle you are looking for:

- Short- or long-wheelbase
- Pick-up or Hard Top body style
- Van or Station Wagon interior

Then look at engine preferences:

- Four-cylinder petrol engine
- Non-turbo diesel
- Diesel Turbo
- Tdi
- Td5
- V8 petrol

After this, consider whether any of the following specialist types are important:

- Ex-military
- Specialist off-roader
- Expedition-equipped
- Camper conversion

Usage

It is not always easy to define in advance just how a Land Rover will be used. You may well imagine you'll just want it for everyday transport, but

enthusiasm grows and has a habit of changing things. It helps greatly if you know from the outset that you will want to engage in:

- Serious off-roading
- Occasional greenlaning
- Family camping trips
- Long-distance touring
- Caravanning
- Carrying heavy work loads
- Commuting, school-runs, and shopping

Budgets

It is crucial to have a definite financial limit beyond which you won't go, whatever the temptation. Unfortunately, a major problem when buying coil-sprung Land Rovers is that their values are higher than other 4x4s of similar age. It means that, while you're buying all the advantages of Land Rover,

There are plenty of Defenders looking for new owners, but condition varies greatly and they hold their value much more strongly than most other vehicles. It pays to have plenty of time available, because finding the right Defender in the right condition, at the right price, is not easy. (Dave Barker)

This is what the battle-ready 90 looks like. With a full roof rack, winch, off-roading tyres and under-body protection you are ready for anything! However, when buying a Land Rover like this it is vital to bear in mind that it has already led a hard life. (Dave Barker)

your financial situation might force you to select an older vehicle, or one in worse condition, than you had hoped.

The unwary buyer on a tight budget is tempted to spend to the limit on a vehicle which requires substantial renovation, either innocently or, more often the case, because logic disappears rapidly when most of us go into buying mode.

There's little point in finding you can't use your new Land Rover until the chassis, engine, and gearbox have received essential attention, but, because you've spent all your cash, you can't afford to get it done, or haven't the time or ability to do it yourself.

Another problem is the failure to appreciate fully, or to close your eyes to, the fuel consumption of one of the largest, heaviest, and least aerodynamic private vehicles on the road. If you're new to four-

wheel-drive machinery, make proper allowance for running costs, especially if the Land Rover is to be used as a general family car. For example, the V8 engine option in the original One Ten always made it a very attractive vehicle, and now they are among the cheapest of the Defender family, but fuel consumption can be as high as 10mpg. It was slightly better after the five-speed gearbox was introduced – but not much.

Even the 300 Tdi, Land Rover's best engine until the Td5 came along in 1998, will not give more than about 27mpg, while very few Td5 drivers get better than 28mpg. With virtually all family cars returning better than 30mpg, and some beating 40mpg, the difference over 15,000 miles (24,000km) of family motoring each year is considerable.

On the other hand, parts prices are relatively low, and all spares are easily available, while insurance costs, too, can be refreshingly modest.

Service and maintenance costs are high when carried out by franchised dealers, and still relatively expensive at specialist workshops. However, much of the routine work is within the capability of most mechanically inclined owners.

Wheelbase

Many first-time buyers make the mistake of thinking it doesn't really matter whether they choose a 90 or 110, only to discover later they've gone for the wrong one. And it's not only beginners who make this mistake; in a rush of enthusiasm for a particular vehicle, even experienced enthusiasts sometimes fall into the trap of buying the wheelbase type which doesn't best suit their needs, and end up with a compromised vehicle.

The fact that buyers can choose between two wheelbases and a variety of body types means that when buying a Defender there really is no need at all to opt for a machine which doesn't suit you in all respects.

The 90 is deservedly the most popular with enthusiasts because the short wheelbase makes it ideal for off-roading, and its square-cut good looks have become the fashion statement of the Land Rover movement. Because of that popularity, and the tendency to want to 'join the gang', some buyers choose a 90 without appreciating that a 110 would suit their needs better.

Of course, if you want to get fully into off-roading, and it's important for your enthusiasm to be on show for all to see, you'll want a 90, which is superior to the 110 in extreme situations because of its shorter wheelbase, much reduced rear overhang, and tighter turning circle. But for most off-roading purposes there's nothing at all wrong with a 110, and it's much better suited for expeditions, camping, and long-distance touring. The 110 is the only Defender which can truly be described as a family vehicle. Although a pair of forward-facing seats can be fitted into the back of a 90, access to them is awkward, and they leave virtually no luggage space. A 90 is fine for a couple of adults, and its universal popularity is very justly deserved, but it is not at all suitable for carrying children, although some families manage it all the same.

There's also the extra-long 130, the basis for some specialist conversions, but more usually seen in the form of the Crew Cab pick-up truck, an

excellent and versatile machine. However, the 130 is much less common than the 90 or 110.

Body type
The type of body matters a great deal to some users, and not at all to others. Before you start looking in earnest give serious consideration to the way the Land Rover will be used, and by whom.

County Station Wagon or Station Wagon variants offer considerable luxury when viewed alongside 'working' Land Rovers, although you don't get the plush carpeting and interior trim which is fitted to the Discovery and Range Rover. This is the best choice (in 110 form) for family car duties and long-distance touring, but is too good if heavy-duty off-roading is intended. It also carries a price premium.

The Hard Top or van body is the most popular because of its versatility. Used in its basic form it is

The 110 County Station Wagon is the best Defender choice for those who want to enjoy family motoring in comfort. This is the most civilised model in the entire range. (Nick Dimbleby)

ideal for off-roading and general load carrying, while common improvements include the fitting of side windows, sound/heat insulating linings and, sometimes, rear seats. They are often better value than Station Wagons, with the added advantage of customising potential.

Pick-up or Truck Cab types are built strictly as working vehicles, but have a charm of their own. They are very good for off-roading, but secure compartments need bolting or welding into the truck bed to hold tools and equipment. They are strictly two-person vehicles (with the exception of the Crew Cab 130), and, with both 90 and 110 wheelbases, are in good supply.

Ex-military

Many of the world's armed services and police forces have made good use of the great family of Defender vehicles since their inception. Along with the usual choice of wheelbase, taking the ex-military route can give you the additional option of

soft-top bodywork. They can be very good value, although you may well end up with 24-volt electrics.

Engines

A surprising number of engines have been used to power Defenders and their predecessors since the advent of the One Ten in 1983. However, not all have suited these otherwise excellent vehicles. A full appraisal of the qualities, shortcomings, fuel consumption, and reliability of all nine engine types is given in Chapter 9, but the information below forms part of the outline information package with which all would-be buyers should arm themselves.

Original choice was either the good old 3.5-litre

Ex-military vehicles are usually worth checking out, especially if you are on a tight budget, because most have been very well maintained mechanically, although bodywork condition varies greatly. (Nick Dimbleby)

petrol V8 or the venerable 2,286cc four-cylinder petrol and diesel units carried over from the Series III, and the Series IIA before that. The V8, of course, is also an old engine, but has always been an excellent power unit, albeit a very thirsty one.

The 2.5-litre diesel and petrol engines followed, before the 2.5 petrol option was dropped and the diesel acquired a Garrett turbocharger, becoming the Diesel Turbo. Then came the first of the Tdi family, the 200 Tdi, which in turn was followed by the 300 Tdi and finally the five-cylinder Td5.

Other than the Td5, which is a completely new-generation unit with an excellent mix of power, torque, and refinement, the best of these units for most people is the 300 Tdi. This had the same power and torque as the 200 Tdi from which it was developed, but was more reliable and less noisy.

The original turbocharged engine, the Diesel Turbo, has been described as 'the worst engine made by Land Rover', but this is unjust. True, the Diesel Turbo proved to have long-term reliability problems, and was never in the same league as the first of the Tdis, but the fact that a Ninety or One Ten has one of these engines should not in itself put you off if the price is right.

Non-turbo 2.5-litre diesels are now quite rare in civilian vehicles, although numerous ex-military 90s and 110s have them. If you can put up with the lack of pace and, again, the asking price is appropriate, don't be put off. It is, in fact, a pretty good off-road engine.

The V8 is, in these days of very high fuel prices, a specialist engine because of its great thirst. However, if an LPG conversion can be justified, running costs work out much the same as for a Tdi.

Engine rundown

Td5: Excellent all-round, but only found in late-model, expensive, vehicles.

300 Tdi: Best of the Tdi engines.

200 Tdi: Some long-term reliability worries, but still going strong in a great many good-value vehicles.

V8: Great thirst, but best for heavy-duty towing.

Diesel Turbo: Long-term reliability problems, but now found in inexpensive vehicles. Good off-road engine.

The 3.5-litre V8 engine was fitted as a standard unit for several years. It is the most appealing engine in many ways, but be prepared for 14-16mpg fuel consumption. Sometimes it is even worse than that. (Dave Barker)

Non-turbo 2.5 diesel, 2.25 diesel, 2.5 and 2.25 petrol: The 2.5 diesel's not too bad, although slow, and the 2.5 petrol, which was a pretty good engine, is now rare. The rest are best left alone, except when the vehicle's very cheap and an engine transplant is viable.

Buying

Where to buy

There have never been so many sources for used Land Rovers, although this presents its own problems. Knowing just where to begin the search can be one of the most difficult parts of the whole exercise. They turn up just about everywhere, although there's a tendency for particular types of Land Rover, or Land Rovers which have been used for specific purposes, to be sold at clearly identifiable places, and advertised through particular publications.

Generally speaking, there's a greater risk when buying any vehicle privately, because there's very little, if any, comeback if the vehicle is subsequently found to have been misrepresented. Despite this risk, however, private advertisements in local papers can be the source of good, honest machines, and it also pays to look for them in less obvious places – a number of years ago I spotted a Range Rover for sale in *Horse & Hound* and, after checking it out, bought for a very fair price what turned out to be a truly excellent five-year-old vehicle.

The principal sources are:

Land Rover franchised dealers: Vehicles are covered by a good warranty and nearly always in excellent order. But they are only ever very recent vehicles, and are always higher-priced than elsewhere.

Specialist Land Rover dealers: Although usually described and sold honestly, not everything you're told should be taken at face value. Asking prices can be ambitious, sometimes excessively so for specialist vehicles such as ex-Camel Trophy.

General used car dealers: Occasionally the source of gems, although you need to watch out for badly neglected ex-farm Land Rovers which have been traded-in. Prices range from fair to 'you must be joking'.

General 4x4 traders: These can be a good source, and it's always an encouraging sign if a vehicle on offer was traded for a more modern or higher specification one by the previous owner. Prices are usually reasonable.

Auctions: Here you take the greatest risk for the chance of the best bargain. Auctions are the place to go if you know what you're looking for and how to check it out. Prices are usually very good.

Local newspapers: Land Rovers privately owned,

Specialist dealers are usually the best source of used Land Rovers. This late-model 300 Tdi was spotted at Four plus 4 in Leeds, and represents the best of the Tdi Defender range. (Dave Barker)

but not necessarily by enthusiasts, often find their way into local papers. However, as with all private sales it is crucial to check legal ownership as well as the condition of the vehicle. Prices can be good because bargaining is often fruitful.

Trader publications: These are the biggest single source of used Land Rovers, but are also the place that some people try to unload unhealthy/dodgy machines. They are nevertheless really worth trying, although you'll look at loads before buying. Prices are all over the place.

Specialist Land Rover magazines: These are not the Mecca for private sales you'd imagine, although they are the place to look for fully-prepared off-roaders and expedition vehicles being sold privately, and for specialist and ex-military dealers. Prices for some private sales can be very ambitious.

Ex-military dealers: The place to go for a Land Rover released from the military but not yet civilian registered. Mostly, they are very honest people and prices are reasonable. Beware, though, because some released Land Rovers are in awful condition.

Checkout

Before examining a vehicle talk to the vendor about how it has been used, when it last changed hands, what work has been carried out, and why it is being sold. Clearly, this applies more to private sales, but it is worth asking the same questions even if it's a dealer sale, because sometimes much of the history is known.

Inspect the paperwork carefully, checking that the name of the registered keeper on the V5 'log book' tallies either with the identity of the person selling it or, if it's a dealer sale, what you're being told. Note how long the vehicle has been owned by the vendor (or currently registered owner). If it is only a short time – less than a year – you need to know why it is being sold so quickly.

Look for proof of purchase, and inform the vendor you'll carry out a check for outstanding hire purchase, etc, with a company such as AA Data Check or HPI. This will tell you if there are any prior claims on ownership and whether it is logged as having been an insurance write-off.

Ask to see previous MoTs, which are a very reliable check on the mileage displayed on the

distance recorder, and see if there's evidence of regular servicing and repairs. Many Land Rovers are maintained by enthusiastic owners, and there may be no paperwork to support their hard work, but vehicles which have been dealer maintained should have the evidence to support it.

If the vehicle's reasonably new, and certainly if it is being sold by a Land Rover dealer, the service book should be fully stamped up, and there should also be invoices for additional work.

Initial inspection

An initial, general look around will tell you much about the vehicle, the way it has been used, and the amount of care it's received. It's worth doing this before checking it out in detail because a preliminary check will sometimes tell you it's not worth spending any more time on it.

Never buy a vehicle if the vendor cannot produce the V5 registration 'logbook'. If you are told it has been sent for, either arrange to come back when it has arrived, or walk away altogether. (Dave Barker)

Land Rovers which are used off-road inevitably pick up some knocks and dents along the way, although it should not stop you buying if everything else is satisfactory and the price is right. This example shows damage to the gearbox crossmember. (Dave Barker)

Does it look genuinely clean, or does it show signs of having been hurriedly washed down for your visit? Walk around the Land Rover and look along the panels and the sill area beneath the doors. A few dents are inevitable with older vehicles, but lots of dents and gouges may well indicate a hard life off the tarmac, or careless ownership.

Is the interior tidy? If it has carpets and they are scuffed and muddy it has most likely been off-roading, and/or not enjoyed the benefit of overmats. Are the seats dirty or torn? Is the headlining intact? Is the dashboard clean, or covered with dirt?

A badly rusted rear crossmember will almost certainly mean MoT failure and must be replaced. Some surface rusting is inevitable on older vehicles, but never forget that this part of the chassis takes all the strains of towing. (Dave Barker)

The fact that Land Rovers are constructed with aluminium alloy body panels does not mean there is no chance of corrosion. Electrolytic reaction between the body skin and supporting steel frame causes corrosion like this, especially on door bottoms. (Dave Barker)

Open the bonnet and look around. If it is filthy, with wires hanging loose, it has been neglected. Low coolant and hydraulic levels, along with pitch black oil on the dipstick, perhaps at a low level, tell the same story (although the oil in diesel engines blackens very quickly).

A Land Rover which fails these initial tests isn't worth buying. There are plenty about, so walk away – but if the early signs are encouraging, dig deeper.

History

It helps to know how the vehicle has been used in the past. Some Station Wagons are used as crew buses on large construction sites, and have a tough time of it. Boating enthusiasts often use Land Rovers for hauling vessels up slipways, with frequent immersion in salt water. And although Land Rovers are designed for off-road use, too

The earliest One Tens had Series III type doors which were in two pieces and had sliding windows. Wind-up windows were introduced concurrently with the launch of the Ninety in 1984, and one-piece doors came a little later. (Dave Barker)

much of it causes premature wear to most mechanical components, puts great strain on steering, suspension parts, and wheel bearings, leads to premature chassis rusting, and plays havoc with the interior.

On the other hand, a Land Rover which has been used for everyday family transport or as a status-symbol company car is unlikely to present any of

This is one of the front coil springs of a 90. The low-rate (or 'softness') and long-travel design transformed the comfort of Land Rover utility vehicles and made them unbeatable off-road. (Dave Barker)

these problems. But if it has clocked up a high mileage in a short time, it is likely to have been driven flat out from dawn to dusk, leading to the possibility of premature engine wear.

Chassis

The most important part of any Land Rover is the chassis, an enormously strong box-section construction which, although resisting the passage of time well, inevitably falls victim to rust over the years. Original chassis are not galvanised, although some replacements are.

The chassis must be inspected very carefully. Look first for dents and gouges caused by contact with rocks off-road. The odd dent is to be expected, especially on older models, but lots of them point to a very hard life. Damage like this turns readily to rust, so look for corrosion or, much worse, evidence of filler, which is totally unacceptable. Repair sections or plates welded into position are okay, but bear in mind that if a chassis has got to the point where entire sections have already been repaired, a full replacement will not be too far away. And that's a big, expensive job.

The rear of the chassis can be more prone to corrosion than the front, while the rear crossmember frequently rusts before the main chassis rails. This is a principal load bearing section, and takes all the stresses of towing, so must be in perfect order. Outriggers, too, rust quite readily, especially those at the bulkhead.

From the point of view of the corrosion inspection, the bulkhead can be included with the chassis. Although it is more than likely that any serious rust will be restricted to the footwell area, which is relatively easy to repair, it is possible that

The steering swivel assembly protects the complex inner mechanisms from everyday road dirt, winter mud, and the rigours of off-roading. Eventually, the chrome-plated swivels become pitted and then start to leak lubricant; examine closely before buying. (Dave Barker)

the bulkhead itself is corroded on very early vehicles. Check from inside the cab and from beneath and above the engine bay. Bulkhead replacement is a major exercise.

Bodywork

The body skin is aluminium alloy, which doesn't rust but is subject to corrosion as the result of electrolytic action where the alloy is in contact with steel. This happens on quite recent vehicles – although it shouldn't – and shows itself as bubbling beneath the paint and crumbly white powder. Virtually all Defenders will display some degree of this corrosion at various points around the body. If it's relatively slight it can be ignored, but extensive bodywork corrosion will need remedial work at some time, which may well include some reskinning and replacement of the underlying steel framework.

The doors should be inspected closely, starting with the hinges and working all the way round, inside and out. The earliest One Tens had Series III-type two-piece front doors, with sliding glass. These are worth retaining if you buy one of these now-rare vehicles, but they don't wear very well and are likely to need complete replacement at some time.

The rear doors take a lot of punishment from road dirt and badly secured loads, while the hinges wear prematurely if the spare wheel is rear-door mounted. Very often, rear window wash-wipers and heating elements don't work, so check them.

Suspension

Land Rover suspension is extremely tough, but with older vehicles, and those which have done a lot of off-roading, or have regularly carried very heavy loads, some problems can be expected. The bushes throughout the system wear, leading to a general sloppiness which is readily noticed during a test drive. Fortunately, replacement is not particularly expensive, and is something anyone buying an older coil-sprung Land Rover should be prepared for.

The springs are huge, tough units which stand the test of time well, but will inevitably lose their strength eventually. If the Land Rover sags on one

Prop shaft universal joints take a pounding on any vehicle which uses them, but they have a particularly tough life on Land Rovers which are used off-road. Use of low ratios imposes high torque levels, while immersion in mud and sand can cause premature wear. (Dave Barker)

side, or sits down at the front or rear, or has a general soggy, woolly feel to the ride and handling, it may well need new springs and shock absorbers. Fortunately again, springs are not expensive and, along with the dampers, are easy to replace.

An important part of the rear suspension on some 110-inch vehicles – but not fitted to all of them – is the Boge self-levelling strut. It is self-energising and is designed to permit full rear suspension travel even when heavily loaded. It is difficult to test accurately because the unit only works when the vehicle is moving, but, depending on the general state of the coil springs, you may be able to notice if the rear of the Land Rover droops noticeably with a couple of people sitting as close as possible to the rear door as you drive along. The self-leveller can be dispensed with, in which case higher-rate rear springs are needed, unless the vehicle is not going to be heavily loaded.

Steering

Another cause of poor handling is wear in the steering system, usually the ball joints, although it can be difficult to decide, without jacking the vehicle up, whether the sloppiness is caused by steering, suspension, or both. In most cases it's both! However, worn steering joints, or even wear in the steering box itself, is no reason to turn away from an otherwise good Land Rover.

While checking the steering, it is important to examine the chrome-plated front swivels. With time these develop surface pitting, particularly after plenty of off-roading in abrasive conditions, causing leaking to occur. The only cure is replacement.

The power steering system is tough, but should be checked for leaks before and after the test drive, and for noise-free operation on the move.

Transmission

Some free-play is to be expected in the permanent four-wheel-drive transmission, mostly coming from gradually developing wear in the propshaft universal joints, but eventually it becomes unacceptable. If it's bad you'll notice clunks and free play as you take up the drive when starting off and when changing gear. If you're not sure when test driving, replicate heavy traffic by travelling slowly in first gear, on and off the throttle; this is when the wear is most annoying and inconvenient.

Wear develops right through the system, and with a differential on each axle plus one between the front and rear propshafts, plus the transfer gearbox, let alone the main gearbox and front constant velocity joints, there are plenty of places for things to go wrong.

Test for smooth changes in all gears by going up and down through the gearbox, and check that it doesn't jump out of gear when accelerating and on the over-run. Select low ratios and repeat the exercise, but don't be too alarmed if the high-low selector is rather stiff in operation, particularly on

There are plenty of Ninetys and One Tens around with the Diesel Turbo engine. Some are terribly tired while others have survived well, so a close visual and aural check is essential, as is a lengthy test drive. (Dave Barker)

a vehicle where there's been no need to use low ratios. Engage the diff lock, the operation of which is confirmed by a warning light on the dash, but don't drive around on any firm surface with the diff lock engaged: this can cause serious transmission damage.

Make sure the handbrake will hold the vehicle on an incline, but don't apply it on the move. Land Rovers have transmission brakes, in the form of a drum brake on the rear prop shaft, and must be used only at a standstill.

Check beneath the vehicle for oil leaks from the axle differentials and main and transfer gearboxes.

Engine

Clearly, the older the vehicle the more allowance must be made for age, and the basic characteristics of the unit. For example, the 2.5 non-turbo and its turbocharged development used in the Diesel Turbo are both noisy and unrefined compared with the 200 Tdi, while the 300 Tdi is even quieter and smoother.

The 2.5 diesel and 2.5 Diesel Turbo are both reliable engines, although the Diesel Turbo has been unfairly labelled as a particularly unsatisfactory unit. It is true, though, that many Diesel Turbos have failed to reach much more than 65,000 miles (105,000km) or so without major overhaul.

With both these pre-Tdi engines check carefully for serious oil leaks, particularly from seals, and with the Diesel Turbo look for oil blown into the air cleaner, and evidence of cracks in the head or block (water in the oil, and oil in the coolant).

The 2.5-litre diesel engines have timing belts, and if there is no hard evidence of belt replacement recently, budget for doing it if you buy the vehicle. Whenever there's doubt, timing belts should always be replaced – it's a great deal less costly and less inconvenient than rebuilding most of the engine if it fails the first time you drive it.

Most, if not all, of these older diesels usually blow out a cloud of blue or white smoke on start-up, but this should disappear quickly. If it persists, there's trouble.

On the move the non-turbo diesel will be noisy and sluggish, while the Diesel Turbo is noisy and

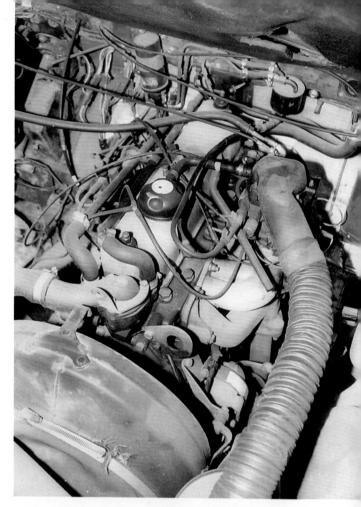

While the original 2.3 petrol engine was inadequate, the 2.5-litre unit derived from it was somewhat better and is quite usable even today. This 2.5 is still working hard on an everyday basis. (Dave Barker)

fairly lively. If the latter fails to accelerate reasonably well (bearing in mind its 0–60mph or 0–96kph time when new was about 22 seconds), and will not cruise happily at 65mph (105kph), there's something wrong with it. However, don't expect too much, because maximum speed was never better than 75mph (120kph), compared with the 68mph (109kph) of the non-turbo.

The 2.25 petrol engine was the same unit being used in contemporary Series IIIs when the One Ten was launched and, although a reasonably smooth engine, it was always a little rattly and inclined to puff out a bit of blue smoke.

Listen for timing chain rattle, and check for excessive crankcase pressure by looking for smoke, as opposed to wispy fumes, from the oil filler cap. Again, as with the diesels, some blue exhaust smoke is to be expected on start-up and very often on the over-run. The engine was built to run on leaded petrol, and will now require either lead replacement fuel, or the use of approved lead replacement additives with unleaded petrol.

The short-lived 2.5-litre petrol engine was similar in many ways, although more powerful and more suited to the vehicle. These are found only rarely, and should be checked out in the same way as the smaller engine.

Smoothest and quietest of the lot was the 3.5-litre petrol V8, but most have deteriorated with age. In good order the V8 should be quiet and smooth at tickover, building to a lusty roar at high revs. Unfortunately, many have suffered from poor maintenance, something they don't like at all; if a V8 runs rough, this is probably why, and if it's smoking as well the wear has spread to pistons, rings, bores, and bearings. A rebuild can be expensive.

Best all-round engines for the entire Defender family are the Tdis. Both are excellent engines, with ideal power and torque characteristics for the host vehicles. They provide perfectly acceptable road-going performance, and excel in off-road situations. Many have been retro-fitted into pre-Tdi Ninetys and One Tens, so they can crop up in the earliest of the family.

Some 200 Tdis have developed quite advanced wear at around 65,000 miles (105,000km) or so, while far more have gone on past 150,000 miles (240,000km) without protest. Some of the premature wear can be blamed on use, so it is worth finding out as much as you can about the way the Land Rover has been driven. For example, some people have chosen Defenders as company cars, perhaps switching from much faster BMWs and Volvos in order to display something different in the company car park. In many cases, drivers have tried to compensate for the relatively poor

The 200 Tdi was a great improvement over the Diesel Turbo, both in performance and economy, as well as reliability. Many 200 Tdis in regular use have completed more than 150,000 miles without overhaul, although a few have expired very much earlier; mostly, they are well worth having. (Dave Barker)

performance by accelerating to full revs for every gearchange and driving the engine flat out on the open road. Sometimes, this has proved too much, particularly for earlier Tdis. Consequently, be on the lookout for engines which have developed valve and piston wear (blue exhaust smoke and/or serious oil leaks), turbocharger wear, intercooler problems, and cracked blocks and heads.

Timing belt changes are, of course, crucial. Find out when one was last done. Many vehicles with 300 Tdi engines have required a modification to the timing belt drive pulleys because of a production fault which caused the belt to run slightly out of line. Other than this, the 300 Tdi has proved more reliable long-term than the 200 Tdi, and problems are few.

The five-cylinder Td5 diesel engine was introduced in 1998, bringing unprecedented power and refinement to diesel-powered Land Rovers. The engine itself is successful, but buyers intending to indulge regularly in extreme off-roading, especially where it involves a lot of deep water wading, need to be aware that Td5

Defenders have a sophisticated electronic engine management system, and that ECUs and their associated components do not mix well with water.

Interior

The seating in the Defender family is either of the hard-wearing cloth used as standard in Station Wagons, or is the less appealing vinyl-covered type found in the utility models. Paradoxically, the cloth is often the longer living of the two because of its greater resistance to tearing, but the fact that the plastic type can be hosed down gives it the practical edge when there's a lot of mud about.

Many enthusiast owners fit waterproof overcovers – an excellent way of preserving cloth seats if the Land Rover is used on a farm or construction site or is off-roaded – but take a good look at the condition of the seats beneath the covers.

Many 300 Tdi engines have required a modification to the cambelt pulley system to overcome a fault in some (but not all) of these engines which caused premature cambelt wear and the risk of belt breakage. (Nick Dimbleby)

Introduced in late-1998 the Td5 diesel engine has won many friends, especially among owners who regularly cover high mileages. The electronic management system raises a question mark over off-road activities which involve regular immersion in very deep water. (Dave Barker)

'Working' Land Rovers usually have no carpeting, but if you're looking at Station Wagons check the state of the carpets. Nearly all Land Rovers leak rainwater at various points around the roof and side windows, and this doesn't do the carpets and seats much good. Condensation is also a problem, especially with basic van-type bodywork not fitted with headlinings or sidewall insulation.

Spotter's guide

1983
One Ten introduced. Bodywork virtually identical to later models, but first-year vehicles easily identifiable by their two-piece, Series III-type front doors with horizontally sliding windows. Wheel arch eyebrows were all body-coloured. Five body types: soft-top; Hard Top; pick-up; High-Capacity Pick-up; Station Wagon/County Station Wagon. Engines: 2,286cc petrol; 2,286cc diesel; 3,528cc V8 petrol. Transmissions: Five-speed permanent four-wheel drive or optional selectable four-wheel drive with four-cylinder engines; four-speed permanent four-wheel drive with V8.

1984
2,495cc diesel replaces 2,286cc. Selectable four-wheel drive option deleted. Ninety introduced with 2,286cc petrol and 2,495cc diesel engines.

1985
V8 engine option for Ninety introduced. Five-speed LT85 gearbox with LT230 transfer box replaces four-speed transmission on V8. 2,495cc petrol engine replaces 2,286cc

1986
SU carburettors replace Zenith on V8. 2,495cc Diesel Turbo introduced.

1987
Wheel arch eyebrows black on utility vehicles, but remain body-coloured on Station Wagons. V8 deleted from Ninety.

1990
Range becomes known as Defender. 200 Tdi introduced. Power steering standard on all models.

1992
V8 deleted from 110 (special order option only).

1994
300 Tdi replaces 200 Tdi. R380 gearbox introduced.

1995
Freestyle option pack introduced.

1998
2,492cc five-cylinder Td5 engine introduced, replacing 300 Tdi. Electronic traction control introduced on Defenders. V8 50 limited edition introduced with 3.9-litre injected engine, exterior roll cage, and four-speed automatic transmission.

Running a Defender

Unless it is used purely as a working vehicle, it's difficult to own a Land Rover without becoming to some degree a Land Rover enthusiast. Either that, or you tire of it rapidly and part-exchange it for a normal car as soon as possible.

People have been using Land Rovers as everyday transport since they first appeared, and there are many owners of Series IIs, IIAs, and IIIs who enjoy the daily ride to work in vehicles which, by today's standards, are slow, noisy, and lacking in creature comforts. However, a Defender, or one of its earlier relatives, makes an excellent commuting machine, especially so when powered by one of the Tdi engines. Only the relatively high fuel consumption takes some of the pleasure from the experience, while its height precludes it from entering many multi-storey car parks.

That same machine which takes you to work during the week assumes a new identity at weekends, when it becomes the ultimate leisure vehicle. It can take you to places inaccessible to others, it can tow a caravan of any size, it can take you greenlaning, or you can pack it with camping gear. You can haul a double horsebox and be sure of getting out of gymkhana fields even if it rains, and you can tow a boat down to the coast and then launch and recover it with ease. Try doing most of these things with the average hatchback.

The engines in detail

In the previous chapter there's plenty of advice on choosing and buying a Land Rover, but anyone who has not had the use of one before, or whose experience has been restricted to earlier Range Rovers or any of the leaf-sprung models, needs to be aware of the very considerable differences

Enthusiasm usually follows rapidly after buying your first Land Rover, and this leads, among many other things, to the annual trek to Billing Aquadrome, Northampton, for the Land Rover festival. (Nick Dimbleby)

which exist in the Defender family when it comes to living with one.

As stated in Chapter 8, it really does make sense to give serious consideration as to how the vehicle will be used and, in conjunction with your purchase and running budget, to decide on the age of vehicle you can afford, and which engine option makes the most sense for your particular circumstances.

Of all these considerations, the engine/vehicle age combination will have the greatest impact on subsequent enjoyment of the vehicle and its running costs. With many used cars it doesn't always make the most sense, financially, to buy the latest you can afford. However, anyone investing in a Defender is wise to opt for the most up-to-date they can afford because of the much better performance and fuel economy available from the later engines. To enjoy a Defender to its fullest potential it is crucial to make the correct engine choice.

Many of us, however, have no option but to buy earlier vehicles, so the advice given here about engines must include those used in the first of the line, the original One Ten, as well as the latest. After all, there's little point in buying, say, an early One Ten because that's all you can afford, only to find that it is too slow, or perhaps too thirsty, to be of any real use.

Other than engines and gearboxes the vehicles have not changed in most significant respects since they were introduced in 1983. The seats have improved a little, the early two-piece front doors disappeared quickly, interior trim and various details have become better, but essentially a 1995 Defender is little different from one produced ten years earlier.

However, the engine development has been unprecedented in Land Rover's history, and probably has no equal anywhere in the car-making world. It's the engines which make all the difference, and no less than nine different power units have been used in the 17 years from 1983 to 2000. These range from terribly inadequate to

It is extremely important to know in advance the sort of driving you will be doing in a Defender before making any purchase decisions. (Nick Dimbleby)

superb, and from the economical to the unaffordably thirsty, and Land Rover utilities can be bought today with any of these power options at prices ranging from about £1,500 for a very early 2.25 diesel One Ten to £24,000 for a recent Td5 110 County Station Wagon.

This is what you can expect from each of the nine engines.

Four-cylinder petrol

As has been stated, the One Ten and Ninety both began life with the already venerable four-cylinder 2,286cc engine which had powered the Series II, IIA, and III. It had improved slightly with age, and acquired better long-term reliability with a five-bearing crankshaft in 1980, but it was not at all a suitable engine for the new vehicles. There aren't many coil-sprung Land Rovers around with these engines now, but they do come up from time-to-time and, because they're cheap, can be attractive to anyone on a tight budget.

Power output as used in the One Ten was a mere 74bhp at 4,000rpm, with 120lb/ft of torque at 2,000rpm. The only true drivetrain advantages with the new Land Rovers were that this meagre power was fed into a five-speed gearbox, compared with the four-speeder of the earlier vehicles, and the transmission was permanent four-wheel drive.

With the five gears, fourth was a little lower than fourth (top) gear on the Series III, and fifth a little higher. It gives little benefit over the earlier vehicle when it comes to maximum speed, just about 70mph (112kph) when the vehicles were new. The ravages of time will have inevitably reduced performance and, anyway, it would be foolhardy in the extreme to push to the limit a 17-year-old engine with an unknown mass of miles behind it. Something is sure to break if that's attempted other than for very short bursts.

The greatest advantage of the fifth gear is that it gives more relaxed cruising, with perhaps the biggest benefit at around 60mph (96kph). This is really as fast as an early One Ten or Ninety fitted with this engine wants to cruise, and can make long motorway journeys somewhat tedious, especially when you take into account the need to change down to fourth for any hill, and sometimes

even for a strong headwind. The good side of this is that at this speed the vehicle feels relatively relaxed, which a Series III never did, and in County models fitted with reasonable soundproofing, or any model with aftermarket sound-deadening material fitted, noise levels are not too bad.

Although these engines can be used for towing – and a great many are in Series III Land Rovers – a caravan hitched up to a well-laden One Ten for a fortnight in Scotland, or on the Continent, will make the unit work very hard. Anyone who is likely to put a Land Rover to this type of use should either buy a Tdi or, if this is not possible, a V8.

The 2,286cc petrol engine (first known as a 2¼ and then, with the One Ten, as 2.3) is not a suitable unit for serious off-roading, either. It suffers the disadvantage of all petrol units whenever there's water around; unless it is waterproofed to the extent employed by the military for its petrol-

The 2,286cc petrol engine was carried over from the Series III, which in turn had taken it from the Series II and IIA. It is reliable and rugged but does not have sufficient power for regular use; the 2.5-litre engine developed from it is better. (Dave Barker)

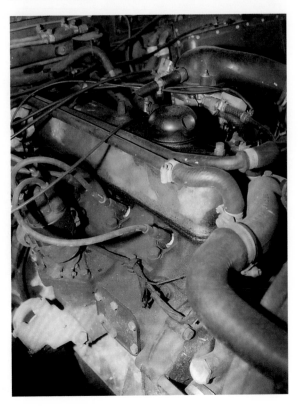

engined Lightweights, it is susceptible to even modest amounts of water. Even with the ignition leads sprayed with silicone and the distributor and coil enclosed in plastic, it doesn't take much to short-out the electrical system at some point, and it can never be used for deep-wading.

This petrol engine is not particularly useful when it comes to steep climbs, especially those which need taking slowly, and awkward rocky sections which require light throttle/high torque treatment. The unit simply isn't responsive enough to cope easily with this sort of terrain.

That's not to say it can't be used off-road, because it can – and, indeed, had proved itself around the world long before the One Ten and Ninety were twinkles in anybody's eyes. For virtually all greenlaning situations the 2,286cc petrol engine is perfectly adequate, and it will pull you through clinging mud, across slippery fields, and up many off-road climbs without difficulty. But if you want to do any heavy-duty off-roading, use something else.

When it comes to four-cylinder petrol engines

you're quite likely to come across the 2,495cc derivation of the old unit, which commenced production in late-Summer 1985. In this engine the power is about 12 per cent better at 83bhp, and the torque is a more respectable 133lb/ft at 2,000rpm. The larger engine was used for all versions of the One Ten and Ninety from Autumn 1985, and is a better alternative than the earlier version. It only adds a few miles per hour on to top speed because, with the very poor aerodynamics of these vehicles, it takes a lot of extra power to squeeze out any more than 70mph (112kph). The comfortable cruising speed is about 65mph (105kph), but there's an improvement in noise levels compared with the 2.3 and, while it doesn't provide the ambience of the V8, it's not at all bad.

This engine is better, too, for all those jobs which the 2.3 struggles with, such as heavy towing,

If you are doing a lot of commuting and other long-distance driving the V8 will cost you dearly because of its great thirst. However, it is the most pleasant of all Land Rover engines. (Nick Dimbleby)

and is a better off-road engine too. It's not perfect, but the differences are there to be admired.

The 2.5 is a longer-living engine than the 2.3, partly because its extra power means it doesn't work quite so hard to do any particular task, but also because it is a more modern unit. Unlike the 2.5-litre diesel with which it is closely related, the 2.5-litre petrol retained chain drive for the camshaft, which adds to its appeal and longevity.

Running costs of all these engines are quite high, and there's the added problem these days that there isn't a type of petrol which fully suits them. On longer journeys, where more use can be made of fifth gear, it's possible to achieve a best consumption figure of about 23mpg, but that's only likely if cruising speed is kept well down. Everyday use, including stop-start town driving, is likely to achieve no better than 18–19mpg.

These are not economical units and a good idea of their thirst can be found in some steady-speed fuel consumption tests carried out on a Series III 88-inch (comparable information with the same engine in the One Ten and Ninety is not available),

in which at a steady 60mph (96kph) the Series III gave 14.8mpg. While a Ninety would be a little better because of its overdrive fifth gear, the difference would not be more than a couple of miles per gallon. Indeed, another test on a Series III, in which the same vehicle was compared with and without a Fairey overdrive unit (which raises the overall gearing, or drops the engine speed, by 21.8 per cent), showed no consumption difference at a steady 60mph, although normal driving on main roads took the average from 17.5mpg without overdrive, to 19.9mpg with it.

Another worry is the use of these engines without leaded petrol, important to prevent valve seat recession. Although a number of lead-replacement additives have been approved for use in Britain and elsewhere, their effectiveness over long-term operation with engines which, of necessity, have to

The pre-turbocharger 2.5-litre diesel is a reasonable engine for off-road use, but is hopelessly out of its depth in modern traffic conditions. The earlier 2,286cc diesel is suitable only for removing to make way for a good engine! (Nick Dimbleby)

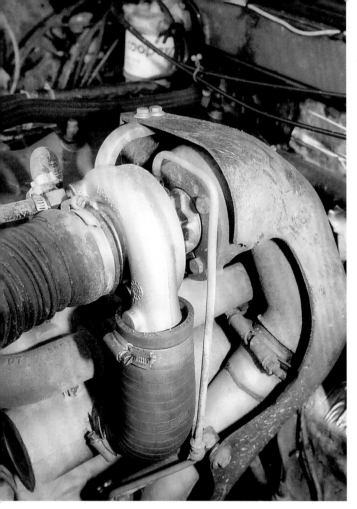

The Diesel Turbo engine is not an attractive unit to look at compared with the Tdis, but it works well enough and was much better than the normally aspirated unit which preceded it. The turbocharger can suffer from lack of lubrication if oil changes are not carried out to schedule. (Dave Barker)

work quite hard, is not clear. The situation is exactly the same with the lead-replacement petrols which are now widely available.

The only good news in this respect is the limited availability in the UK of traditional four-star petrol, a concession made available principally for the historic car movement; but filling stations able to provide it are few and far between. Only 120 sources of leaded petrol were listed throughout Britain in June 2000. (At the time of writing a fully updated list was published in every issue of *Classic Car Weekly*.)

Petrol V8

For many people the V8 is the only engine to have in a Land Rover. It is smooth and powerful and, for some, there's nothing like the burble of a V8 for bringing a tingle to the back of the neck.

The 3.5-litre Rover V8 engine began life with Buick in 1961, so is the longest-lived power unit in Land Rover's line-up. Even the latest versions are descended directly from the American original. It was first used in utility Land Rovers in the Stage 1 Series III 109-inch, and was the star in the original list of engine options for the One Ten in 1983. The V8 continued as an option in the One Ten and Ninety (although it wasn't offered with the first Ninetys) and then for a short while in Defenders. It has been dropped from the production line, though, as Land Rover increasingly standardised on Tdis, and is not available at all with the Td5 series.

In its original form in the first One Tens it came just as it did with the then-current Range Rover, although with less power, and still used four-speed transmission while all the other One Tens had five gears. Even in this form, it was a delightful engine for the One Ten, giving good performance from its 114bhp and 185lb/ft of torque, with an 80mph (129kph) cruising speed which was then simply astonishing in a Land Rover.

The downside was its enormous appetite for fuel, with 12mpg being commonplace, and for most owners this took the edge off the enjoyment. I owned one of the very early One Tens and found its consumption very much worse than the Range Rover – with identical engine and transmission – which followed it. I could get 19 or sometimes 20mpg from the Range Rover, but never more than 14mpg from the One Ten.

The situation improved with the Santana-built five-speed LT85 gearbox introduced in 1985, when the V8 also became part of the Ninety engine list, and it is this combination which most V8 buyers will encounter these days. Because of the V8's thirst and, at least in Britain, extremely high fuel prices, V8 Land Rovers are not as popular as they once were, and to a degree prices reflect this.

If you're not bothered about the fuel cost, or don't plan on doing many miles annually, perhaps using your Land Rover only for recreation, the V8 is still a very worthwhile option. And if you are intending to cover long distances, it's well worth considering an LPG conversion, the cost of which can be recouped in a year or two with LPG being roughly half the cost of petrol.

The V8 engine gives the utility Land Rovers a level of mechanical refinement which isn't possible with any of the diesels, not even the Td5. Along with this there's a top speed of just about 90mph (144kph) and 85mph (137kph) cruising … if you don't mind watching the fuel gauge moving downwards. At 14 seconds acceleration to 60mph (96kph) this is at least three seconds quicker than the Tdi, and there's an overall lustiness about the performance which feels most un-Land Rover-like.

Fuel consumption, however, remains the bugbear of the V8. In a road test of a V8 Ninety in *Autocar* in 1985 the magazine recorded an overall figure of 13.2mpg, commenting that average driving should take it to 14.5mpg, and a gentle approach would extend it to 17mpg.

It's a mistake to buy a V8 Land Rover in the belief that because it's a large-capacity engine it must be reliable. The Rover V8 can indeed be reliable over very high mileages, but only when oil changes and other servicing routines are carried out to the book. Therefore, try to assure yourself that the engine has been properly maintained before you buy, and keep the schedules going religiously afterwards.

In most respects the V8 is a very good off-road engine, although the fact that it needs 2,500rpm to produce maximum torque gives it very different characteristics to, say, the Tdi units – which provide a higher torque figure than the V8 at only 1,800rpm.

Something which many enthusiasts admire about the V8 is its extremely smooth power delivery. When used in conjunction with a stripped-out 90 it has a good power-to-weight ratio. It's universally popular with enthusiasts involved in speed-related off-road competition, when it is normally used in conjunction with automatic transmission.

The big problem with the V8 is the vulnerability of all petrol engines to water, and it takes a great deal of effort to waterproof a V8 satisfactorily … and even then you can never be really sure that a

Defenders are excellent tow vehicles, and many are bought with caravanning holidays in mind. Some are even converted into mobile homes. (Nick Dimbleby)

few drops won't short out one of the plugs, or find their way into the distributor.

Non-turbo diesels

The 2,286cc diesel engine, like the petrol unit of the same size, was carried over into the One Ten. However, it was replaced by the 2.5-litre version in February 1984, so its lifetime in the new vehicle was brief, and it was never used in the Ninety.

That the old diesel was used for a such a short time is a cause for celebration. With only 60bhp available it was never powerful enough for Series IIIs, even though it was a popular choice, but to put it in an all-new Land Rover in the 1980s is something of which Solihull's management should have been ashamed.

Because of its brief use in the One Ten, only a handful of survivors remain. The best thing that

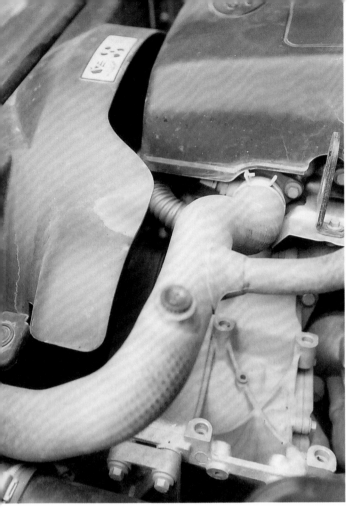

The Td5 engine's complexity can be off-putting to diy enthusiasts, although the management system ensures it retains its all-round tune much more satisfactorily than previous diesels. (Dave Barker)

Land Rover diesels. Having maximum torque so low in the rev range means that towing is not quite as hard-going as the maximum power figure would suggest, while in off-roading situations there's surprisingly good response to limited throttle input. It's a tough, slogging engine capable of pulling a Ninety or One Ten through deep mud, up slippery hills, and over difficult rocky sections with relative ease.

It's on the open road that you notice the limitations which are inevitable with only 67bhp on tap. Maximum speed is just about 70mph (112kph), which is about 10mph (16kph) better than the 2.25 diesel-powered Series III with which it is most frequently compared. It will actually cruise at 70mph, provided there are no inclines and no headwind, and with a decent tailwind will reach 80mph (129kph). To maintain the 70mph cruise, or anything like it, lots of use needs to be made of fourth gear.

The achievement of this engine was to make the new Land Rovers acceptable for road use and to give them the ability to keep up (well, almost) with other traffic. Even when used very hard during a road test for *Motor* in 1986 it returned an overall fuel consumption figure of 21.8mpg, and most owners can expect to get 23mpg in normal use, which is better than the earlier, smaller engine.

Diesel Turbo

The considerably reworked 2.5-litre diesel which emerged as the Diesel Turbo at the end of 1986 provided Land Rover with a crucial shot of adrenalin, and enabled Solihull to hold its head above water in terms of increasingly important diesel power until the first Tdi came along.

Looked at today, the Diesel Turbo appears crude, unsophisticated, noisy, and of questionable reliability, but when it was introduced it was hailed as an important step forward. It was used until the introduction of the Tdi to the Defender in 1990, and the large numbers produced means that plenty are still in use today.

Because the vehicles fitted with this engine are now all more then ten years old, and because of it's acknowledged inferiority to the Tdi, Ninety and One Ten Diesel Turbos are usually very affordable.

can be said is that any of these remaining 2.25-litre diesels are inevitably going to be cheap and, therefore, ideal candidates for engine transplants. Even at a give-away price, to buy a One Ten with this engine with the intention of using it will certainly result in severe disappointment.

The 2,495cc unit was developed from the five-bearing 2,286cc engine without a great deal of effort by Land Rover. The increase in capacity and power was achieved by lengthening the stroke, while a new DPS injector pump provided more accurate fuel metering and helped improve fuel consumption. Cold starting was improved, too, with more advanced glow-plugs.

Yet for all this, maximum power was only 67bhp and torque a modest 114lb/ft, albeit at the extremely useful 1,800rpm which is a feature of

Consequently it's an engine which purchasers at the budget end of the Defender range may well end up with.

In designing the engine – it was far more than a 2.5 with a turbocharger bolted on – Land Rover engineers were much more concerned with pulling power than with outright performance. Yet anybody who has driven both the normally-aspirated 2.5 and the Diesel Turbo cannot fail to be impressed with the difference.

The turbocharged engine boosted maximum speed by about 5mph (8kph) over the non-turbo 2.5, taking it to 75mph (121kph), which is also a realistic cruising speed. The earlier engine would also cruise at maximum speed (as would the engine before it), but it took only the slightest upward slope or headwind to knock it back to 60mph (96kph), whereas although the Diesel Turbo is easily dislodged from 75mph, it will nevertheless keep up 70mph (113kph) with relative ease.

Although there's no rev counter, maximum speed with the turbocharged engine equates to 3,750rpm in fifth gear, just below the peak power

point of 4,000rpm. The engine is governed to 4,250rpm. This gives the Ninety and One Ten quite brisk acceleration to 50mph (80kph), which is reached in 14 seconds. However, so much power is required to accelerate the very un-aerodynamic vehicle beyond this point that it takes a further eight seconds to reach 60mph.

In everyday use, this makes the Diesel Turbo an easy engine to live with in terms of performance and general usefulness, while its low-down lugging ability (quite a breakthrough for Land Rover at the time, considering the general state of turbocharger technology in the early 1980s) makes it a very handy off-road engine.

It may be noisy compared with the Tdi, and the under-bonnet layout really is a mess compared with more modern engines, but it is only the long-

Although the Td5 engine produces its maximum torque at slightly higher engine revolutions than the Tdi, the latest Defender is an excellent off-road machine, particularly when fitted with the optional electronic traction control. (Nick Dimbleby)

term reliability which lets it down in any significant way, especially when you take into account the present-day purchase price of Diesel Turbo Land Rovers. It's principal weak points are the cylinder head, which develops cracks, and the pistons, which are also inclined to crack and, sometimes, to lose chunks altogether.

Despite this, if the engine is in good condition when it's first bought, and is then used with a degree of respect – which means avoiding long spells at near-maximum rpm, paying meticulous attention to coolant temperatures and levels, and always changing the oil at the recommended interval, or before – it should give long and reliable service.

The Tdi engines

There is no doubt that these are the best of all Defender engines prior to the Td5, and that in many respects both the 200 Tdi and 300 Tdi are preferable to the V8 petrol engine. They develop a little more torque than the carburettor-fed 3.5-litre V8, the most important consideration in a Land Rover, and travel nearly twice as far on each gallon of fuel.

The 200 Tdi was a genuine breakthrough when it was first introduced with the launch of the Discovery in 1989. It was an all-new engine, and the first of Land Rover's diesels to feature direct injection, with its advantages of power and economy. It was introduced into the newly named Defenders in 1990, in a slightly lower state of tune than in the Discovery. However, the Defender's 107bhp was only 4bhp less than in the Discovery, and the torque, at 188lb/ft, was 10lb/ft less. According to Land Rover this was done to slightly reduce the stresses when running continuously at maximum rpm in low gears, which they considered a significant feature of the everyday life of Defenders.

The interior of the County Station Wagon is as close as you will get in a utility Land Rover to the trim and comfort levels of the Discovery and Range Rover. But there is no mistaking the functionality of any of the Defender Station Wagons, regardless of the level of equipment.

Whatever the reason, the new engine was significantly more powerful than the Diesel Turbo, and had 25 per cent more torque – improvements which transformed diesel-powered Land Rovers and which, today, make even the earliest 200 Tdi Defender a delightful vehicle to drive.

With Tdi power, Defenders have a maximum speed of 85mph (137kph) and will cruise all day at 75–80mph (121–129kph). The slowing-down effect of hills and headwinds is very much reduced, although a combination of a long motorway incline, headwind, and a heavily loaded vehicle can bring you down to fourth gear.

More than absolute speed, it's the liveliness of the Tdi which impresses the most. The 0–60mph (0–96kph) time is about 17 seconds, which means that although you won't beat hot hatchbacks away from the lights, the Defender is able to mix it with the rest of the traffic and, on the open road, to cruise at the same speed as most other cars. Gone are the days of crawling along in lines of HGVs.

Although owners have towed caravans, horseboxes, and other trailers with all previous diesel engines, the Tdi is the first one to be able to do it with consummate ease. The combination of Tdi engine and Defender weight and size makes it a perfect tow vehicle for caravan touring holidays, as countless owners have been delighted to discover for themselves.

The 200 Tdi is, generally, a reliable unit. Some have developed problems with cracks in their blocks at fairly low mileages (60–70,000 miles, or 96–112,000km) while others have gone on past 200,000 miles (322,000km) with no trouble at all. Mostly, they are reliable for 120,000 miles (193,000km) or so, but top-end overhauls are not uncommon soon after.

The 300 Tdi does not appear to have the same problems. Although performance remains the same, it was considerably re-engineered from the

Pick-up, or Truck Cab versions of the 90 and 110 invariably begin life as working vehicles on farms or construction sites. They are attractive vehicles, but need extra-careful checking because of the risk of prior abuse, and are not the most practical of Land Rover models. (Nick Dimbleby)

200 Tdi and, as well as being quieter and smoother, appears to have no longer-term problems. Both engines, of course, require strict attention to routine service schedules.

One problem which has caused difficulties for 300 Tdi owners has been caused by incorrect alignment of the pulleys for the camshaft drive belt, leading to premature wear and, in some cases, total belt failure with varying degrees of engine damage. This did not affect all 300 Tdi engines, and the units in question have in all probability been rectified by now, although Land Rover has been most reluctant to acknowledge the problem and some dealers have been less than forthcoming with information to their customers.

The new gearbox introduced with the 300 Tdi gave much improved gear selection with more logical gear positions, and is a sweeter unit all-round. At the same time, revisions to the clutch mechanism reduced operating pressures; drivers no longer develop massive muscles in their left leg in stop-start conditions.

The Tdi engines produce commendable economy when one takes into account the shape and weight of the vehicles in which they are fitted, and the fact that many owners work these engines extremely hard in order to make the most of the inevitably limited performance of Defenders. It is quite possible to achieve 25mpg on a regular basis, and as much as 28mpg on long journeys with a little bit of restraint. However, when used very hard consumption can be as much as 22mpg.

The Td5

Significantly smoother than the Tdi and with 122bhp on hand, the 2.5-litre five-cylinder turbocharged engine specially developed by Land Rover has shown yet again that it's not only the giants of car making who can come up with world-class engines. Although it's more powerful, the Td5's 195lb/ft of torque at 1,950rpm is the same as the Tdi's, but at 150rpm more, so there's just a little less punch at very low revs.

The engine is a delight to live with, combining the refinement of saloon car diesels with the power you need in a Land Rover. Economy is just a fraction better than the Tdi, although the difference is too slight to notice on a day-to-day basis. There don't appear to be any reliability problems.

Just about the only drawback when it comes to true enthusiast use is the total dependence on electronic control systems. It's not clear how the electronics will stand up to years of abuse in water, mud, and sand, and for this reason the Td5 is probably not the first choice for anyone who intends doing a lot of serious off-roading. For everyone else, however, the new generation of Defenders with this superb engine are the vehicles to aim for – despite their present high cost.

Body options

Although the type of body and level of trim has less bearing on the pleasure derived from a Defender than making the right engine choice, it helps greatly if you get it right. Clearly, a Pick-up body makes no sense for anyone wishing to use a Defender for family transport, but it is surprising how many people buy a 90 when a 110 would be altogether better, or choose a County Station Wagon when their hobby is off-roading in as much mud as possible.

The County Station Wagon is the easiest to live with and should be the preferred choice for anyone wishing to combine commuting with family holidays. But if finances don't run to full CSW specification, which carries a substantial price premium, it's possible to create your own by buying a basic Hard Top, installing windows, soundproofing, carpets, and headlinings, and then fitting aftermarket seats of your choice into the newly created rear passenger area. This is most commonly done with 90s.

Noisiest of all Land Rovers are Hard Tops in their basic, ex-factory form. The bare sides, rear wheel arch areas and floor transmit noise from the exhaust, transmission, suspension and tyres, and suffer badly from condensation for much of the year – uncomfortably so in winter.

Pick-up bodies appeal to many, especially if working loads need to be carried and there's no family to worry about. However, the open truck bed provides no security for luggage or for off-roading equipment, unless secure steel containers are bolted to the truck floor.

Modification and preparation

Good though the Defender is in its standard specification, a lot can be done to make everyday life with a Land Rover more enjoyable and to prepare it for off-road activities and long-haul expedition work. Whatever you're planning to do with your Land Rover, though, there's usually no need for any sort of modification to Tdi engines, gearboxes, transmissions, or bodywork in order to obtain better performance. However, there is a massive choice of 'bolt-on' equipment for various types of off-roading, including safety fitments such as roll cages, wheels and tyres, and special expedition items. And, uniquely to Land Rovers, it

Greenlaning can be enjoyed in perfectly standard vehicles without risk of damage, provided you are careful to avoid overhanging branches and bramble thickets. It can be altogether different in wet, wintry conditions and considerate enthusiasts avoid known muddy sections to reduce serious disturbance to the track surface. (Nick Dimbleby)

Mud-terrain tyres are available under various brand names and are the best choice for serious off-roading where deep mud is a persistent problem. Otherwise, a less-aggressive, all-terrain tread pattern can be the best bet. (Nick Dimbleby)

is always possible to discard an early type of engine and fit in its place a Tdi or petrol V8, thereby upgrading performance at a stroke.

Greenlaning

For very many green lane outings there's no need to change anything at all on even the most standard Land Rover. This is particularly so during the drier parts of the year when you're unlikely to find any sections bad enough to cause difficulties. Even in the winter months there's plenty of greenlaning which doesn't require special equipment and, because of today's environmental situation and the political sensitivity of many routes, any tracks which might prove particularly

Owners of 90s fitted with rear anti-roll bars find the vehicle's behaviour on the road is much better than non-roll bar Defenders but the bar restricts articulation of the rear axle slightly, so for serious off-roading, it pays to remove it altogether. (Dave Barker)

difficult in bad weather and would result in surface damage should not be driven.

The greatest individual aid to traction for green lane outings is the use of all-terrain or mud-terrain tyres, any enthusiast with a Defender fitted with general-purpose road-biased tyres should invest in a set of tyres more suited for off-road work. It has become fashionable to fit mud-terrain tyres on 4x4s regardless of whether they'll ever be taken off-road, but this is not the most sensible approach. Mud terrains might give the impression you're a hard off-roader, but unless you're likely to have a use for them, it's better to choose a less aggressive tread pattern.

Mud terrains will give you a better chance of coping with deep mud and some (but by no means all) slippery climbs, but there's a downside to them: when being used on wet tarmac the very characteristic of their design which makes them so good in mud – the widely-spaced, large tread blocks – means you have less rubber in contact with the road than with other tyre types. Consequently, stopping distances are increased in wet conditions.

Therefore the sensible tyre choice for anyone likely to go greenlaning without getting involved in very severe conditions is an all-terrain type, with relatively large tread blocks combined with a less-open overall pattern. These tyres are surprisingly effective and are well capable of dealing with most conditions the enthusiast is likely to encounter. Furthermore, they wear better than the mud-terrain type when vehicles are used principally on the road. On the other hand, if your greenlaning and other off-roading activities involve driving in deep mud on a regular basis, it would be pointless to fit any other type of tyre than a mud terrain. Bear in mind, however, that mud tyres are not at all effective in sand.

Some Defenders are fitted with anti-roll bars and drivers who clock up high road-going mileages often ask if they'd be better removing the rear anti-roll fitment. The answer is to leave it in place. The bar gives better handling on the road and, with extensive road use, would be missed if it wasn't

This is the hole in a five-speed gearbox into which the wading plug screws. Wading plugs should be fitted whenever the vehicle is to be used in water or deep mud and, if not removed immediately, should be taken out within a day or two. They must not be left in for normal running, because the hole permits the escape of small quantities of oil. (Dave Barker)

there. Off-road, the anti-roll bar restricts axle articulation, but in most greenlane situations you can avoid requiring the full potential articulation. It's only when your off-roading becomes more demanding that the restriction imposed by the anti-roll bar creates problems.

Wading plugs

One aspect of which owners should be aware is that all Land Rovers have a drain hole in the clutch housing between the engine and gearbox; those which have a camshaft belt drive also have one at the bottom of the drive belt housing. Engines such as the V8, the 2.25 petrol and diesel units, and the 2.5 petrol have chain-driven camshafts which do not require a drain. These holes permit oil to drain away in the event of an oil leak in this area, and should therefore be left clear in normal use.

However, whenever the vehicle is likely to be immersed in water or mud which may reach the drain holes, wading plugs should be screwed in to prevent ingress. It is important to do this because water or liquid mud or sand entering the holes can cause serious damage.

The plugs should be removed afterwards, at the very latest two or three days after they've been fitted. Where vehicles are operated in conditions requiring the continuous use of wading plugs, they should be removed every few days to permit any oil to drain away.

Wading plugs are available from all Land Rover dealers, and many accessory and parts shops, and should be carried in a handy spot inside the Land Rover, along with a 13mm or half-inch spanner.

Serious off-roading

Anyone who plans to use a 90 or 110 for off-roading in demanding conditions needs to ensure the vehicle is properly equipped. Again, the first and easiest 'modification' is to ensure that the tyres are suitable. The choice will almost certainly be the mud-terrain type, of which there are many types available. Check out the relative qualities and

Extreme conditions, especially those involving deep mud, require plenty of expertise and a well-equipped vehicle. In situations like this, mud-terrain tyres, a winch and specialist recovery attachment points are essential. (Nick Dimbleby)

Deep wading such as this can only be done with a vehicle which has been specially prepared. Most important is the fitment of a high-level air intake, or snorkel, and the extension of breather tubes from gearboxes, etc. It is virtually impossible to waterproof a petrol engine to cope with deep water, so diesels win every time. (Nick Dimbleby)

prices of different makes by going to an off-road tyre specialist.

The next consideration should be whether or not to equip the Land Rover for use in water deeper than the non-adapted maximum depth of roughly the height of the uppermost section of the wheel rim. Entering water much deeper than this carries with it a significant risk of it getting into the air intake system and, consequently, damaging the engine. So, if you're ever likely to get serious about off-roading, or you want to be able to cope with water whenever it occurs – such as flooded roads – it really pays to be permanently prepared.

Deep wading is challenging and can be fun, but it can also do a lot of damage and is potentially dangerous. It's wise to equip your Defender so that it can cope with deep water, but it is best to avoid it if at all possible!

Because they have no ignition system diesel engines will keep running in deep water, but only if you have an adequate high-level air intake and a fully-sealed air system. It takes only a tiny amount of water to be sucked in because of inadequate sealing to destroy the engine. Consequently, your first purchase must be a good-quality high-level intake (snorkel) which is suitable for the 2.5-litre turbocharged engine in the Land Rover. It should reach roof height, or slightly more, and must be substantial enough to take the knocks of off-roading. It will need firm attachment to the A-post beside the windscreen.

With the snorkel, buy suitable piping (flexible and solid) to link it to the air filter box, and make sure you have a good supply of high-quality clips

A high-level air intake must extend to the roofline of the vehicle, and all joints between the base of the intake and the inlet manifold, including the edges of the air box, must be totally sealed and checked before every off-roading session. (Nick Dimbleby)

Winch operation must be done with great care, and wherever possible should involve an assistant (the 'winch master') who controls the entire operation from a position where the winch is clearly visible. Winches can be dangerous, while at all times it is crucial to keep well away from winch cables under tension. (Nick Dimbleby)

to secure all joints, possibly using a suitable silicone sealant as well to ensure a total seal throughout the system. The air filter box itself will need additional sealing. Silicone applied round the rim of the base will seal it solidly when the top is in position, but it makes sense to also seal round the join with heat-resistant tape. All the breather tubes from the axles and gearboxes must be extended so they pass up the outside of the snorkel tube.

There's not much more you need to do for occasional deep wading, which should be restricted to wheel arch height if at all possible. You can go deeper – indeed, a diesel Land Rover will run with the engine fully submerged – but then you'll be damaging the alternator and probably the turbocharger.

Virtually nothing can be done to stop water coming in through the door seals, so part of your preparation should be to replace any carpets with rubber mats. If you go really deep you'll soak the seats – even waterproof covers won't protect them if they're under water.

A strong plastic bag, or even an old coat, draped

over the radiator grille, will reduce the flow of water on to the fan, and will also protect the radiator from floating debris or, in winter, chunks of ice. And don't forget to fit those wading plugs!

Diesel-engined Land Rovers are the only type suitable for deep wading because of the absence of a distributor, high-tension plug leads, and spark plugs. Without a high-level air intake Land Rover's maximum wading depth advice must be followed, and even then it is possible that a petrol-engined vehicle might short out. It is extremely difficult to make a petrol engine's electrics fully waterproof.

Given the proper precautions all diesel Land Rovers are capable of similar wading performance. However, great care must be exercised with the Defender Td5 because of its total reliance on a sophisticated electronic management system. It has not yet been fully established whether the management system and its ECU, the electronic traction control (ETC) 'black box' and other electronics will withstand regular immersion, but the general feeling is that they won't. Water-proofing them to a satisfactory level is likely to prove extremely difficult, especially in the case of the management system. You might think you've got away with it after one or two outings, but long-term reliability will almost certainly suffer. The best advice is to forget about serious wading in the Td5; deep water is especially unkind to vehicles bristling with electronics.

The next consideration should be a winch, essential for any serious off-road outings and all expedition work, and very reassuring for even light-hearted greenlane outings. The most popular type is the electric winch, which takes current from the Land Rover's battery (see later) and, via a low-geared electric motor, provides power to the drum on which the steel winching cable is stored. A less well-known alternative is the hydraulic type, such as the Milemarker, which takes its operating power from the vehicle's power steering pump.

Several makes of electric winch are available. All of them are well-made, they all have similar characteristics within certain power bands, and all the models sold in Britain will fit easily to a 90 or 110. In most cases you can buy the winch complete with a winch mounting bar which replaces the front bumper. Alternatively, winches may be mounted on the bumper which, because of its rugged construction and the way it attaches directly to the front sections of the chassis, will comfortably handle all the stresses involved with winching.

When choosing a winch it pays to buy the most powerful available. This is not so much because you will necessarily need all the pulling power it will provide, but because it improves the speed of operation of a heavy recovery. An electric winch operating close to its capacity can be used for only a few minutes before it must be rested to cool it down. If, for example, the winch is only running at half capacity the operating periods will be longer than a fully-loaded unit – but rest intervals will still be needed if the pull is a long one.

An hydraulic winch is also very easily fitted to a Land Rover. The hydraulic pressure which operates it comes from the vehicle's power steering pump via a straightforward adaptation. Although the actual line speed of a top-flight hydraulic winch,

such as the Milemarker, is slower than an equivalent electric type, a long and difficult recovery with a hydraulic unit can actually be faster. This is because the winch does not heat up, so can run continuously until the recovery is complete, and the line speed is constant.

As well as a winch, a Land Rover being prepared for serious off-roading should also be fitted with special recovery attachments at the front (if they're not part of a special winch mounting bar), Most effective are JATE rings, developed originally by the British Army for airborne operations. These are bolted through the longitudinal chassis sections. The towing equipment takes care of rear recovery … but only as long as it is in perfect condition, and

One of the few acceptable forms of heavy recovery is the JATE ring, an extra-strong attachment which should be bolted through the main chassis frames near the front of the vehicle. For heavy-duty recovery they should be used as a pair, connected via a bridle arrangement to equalise forces throughout the chassis. (Nick Dimbleby)

The one weak point of a Land Rover is the upper body, which does not possess the structural strength to withstand a roll over. Many enthusiasts fit full or partial roll cages as a sensible safety precaution while, for competition use, they are compulsory. (Nick Dimbleby)

the rear crossmember and all the chassis are free of rust damage.

Although Land Rovers are exceptionally tough vehicles, the upper body has no structural strength and a roll-over can have nasty consequences. Many enthusiasts now fit roll cages to Hard Top bodies for peace of mind, and if you own, say, an ex-military 110 soft-top a roll cage is highly recommended.

Any soft-top vehicle without a roll cage or rollover bar relies entirely on the windscreen surround to support it and protect its occupants if it turns over. The windscreen structure of a Land Rover is not designed for that purpose, which means the occupants are likely to be crushed if something goes wrong and the vehicle flips on to its top.

When deciding on roll-over protection there's the choice of a full-blown cage or the simpler single-bar anti-roll arrangement. If you're likely to

become involved in competitive trialling at CCV (cross-country vehicle) level you will have to invest in a fully approved roll cage, but for normal use the single-bar type may well suit you best.

Don't be tempted to make one up for yourself with a few lengths of tubing, in the belief that a cheap DIY job will do just as well. It won't, because there's no substitute for the knowledge of metal strengths, stress points and safe design which you get when you buy recognised, professional items.

There are plenty of cages and bars on the market, especially designed for Land Rovers. You can get excellent protection with the single-bar type, the best of which have immensely strong bracing sections for bolting or welding directly on to the chassis; the main bar structure also connects directly to the chassis. With one of these fitted the rollover protection is much better than with a standard Hard Top Land Rover, which is why enthusiasts also fit them to roofed vehicles. For soft-tops, the rollover bar can be supplied to precise dimensions to allow the normal canvas hood to fit snugly over it.

For the ultimate in protection, even if you don't have competition in mind, a tailor-made full roll cages is the answer. Some are made by specialist workshops, although the best-known are the Safety Devices range, with so many variations that you're sure to find just what you want.

Full cages provide a higher degree of safety to driver and passengers – which is why they're compulsory for competition – but are somewhat more expensive and can be considerably more difficult to fit. However, anyone who has examined the roll cage inside a Camel Trophy Discovery needs no further advice on the amount of protection it provides.

Removing and replacing a canvas top will be no more difficult with a roll cage or anti-roll bar fitted. Indeed, most enthusiasts find that the extra support provided by the protective steelwork makes the canvas a little tighter all round, and less inclined to flap when surrounded by lorries on motorways.

The tubing should be wrapped in special impact-absorbing sleeving to protect heads, arms, and bodies from direct contact with the steel in an accident or when bouncing about off-road. This is available from roll cage suppliers.

Cross-axle lockers

One of the few complaints made by off-roading enthusiasts is that Land Rovers are not fitted with any means of locking either or both of the axle differentials in order to maximise traction. Even with the centre differential between the front and rear prop shafts locked a Land Rover will be immobilised in any situation which leads to loss of traction by one wheel on both axles. Being able to lock either of the axle diffs, or having a limited slip arrangement on either or both axles, minimises the chances of becoming stuck.

Fortunately, various aftermarket systems are available, most of which can be home-fitted by competent DIY owners. It is possible, at one extreme, to fit manually operated lockers to both axles or, at the other, to have a limited slip differential operating on just one. The full locking system will get you through just about anything, but even the limited slip diff will make a profound difference to a Land Rover's ability to cope with mud, slippery hills, snow, and ice.

Perhaps the most popular differential

conversion is to fit ARB air lockers, which replace the standard Rover axle differential. Normal diff action is retained until the locking system is activated by a compressed air system, when it forms a solid link across the axle. Most owners fit just one ARB unit, usually to the rear axle, but it is possible to have them front and rear for extreme conditions. The unit is supplied as a complete differential, with the additional option of the compressor and fitting kit.

Another commonly used device is the Torson Gleason differential conversion, which can be used on either or both axles. This again allows normal differentiation while the tyres are gripping, but

These are the dashboard switches for operating an ARB differential lock, which is engaged by air pressure fed from an on-board compressor. The system is extremely effective. (Dave Barker)

proportions the torque according to the available traction whenever grip is lost. It's a good system, but relies on the driver stabbing at the brake pedal whenever grip has been lost and the vehicle has stopped, in order to prompt the unit to transfer torque. It therefore has the disadvantage that in most cases you'll come to a standstill before grip is restored.

A third type is the Detroit Locker, which automatically locks up the differential whenever it senses traction is about to be, or has been, lost. The Detroit unit can only be used on the rear axle, but is most effective in operation and, because it requires no driver input, and doesn't have to wait until the Land Rover has stopped, is one of the most suitable for extreme off-roading.

There's also the Truetrac limited slip differential to consider. This is not a locker, as such, because it never locks an axle as a solid piece but, when one wheel is spinning, it permits sufficient torque to be transmitted to the gripping wheel to pull you through in most cases. The Truetrac may be used on either, or both axles, and for extreme

Many off-road enthusiasts fit under-body guards to protect steering components, differentials and sumps from violent (and often catastrophic) impact with rocks. A wide choice of protection is available and it is all easy to fit on a diy basis. (Nick Dimbleby)

effectiveness can be used on the front with, say, a Detroit locker on the rear.

Other off-roading add-ons

Under-body protection is essential for serious off-roading in order to prevent rocks and other projections damaging the differentials, steering mechanism, sumps, and other vulnerable areas. It is also very advisable to fit steel sill protectors, which are bolted to the chassis and run along each side of the vehicle beneath the doors – an area which takes a lot of punishment in extreme situations. The manufacture and sale of the various guards and shields has become very big business; along with winches and roll cages they have proved popular with owners who want their Land Rovers simply to look the part, as well as those who intend to use them in anger.

Popular under-body items are bolt-on differential guards, steering guards, and axle guards, manufactured either in heavy duty aluminium alloy or steel. All these items, along with sill protectors, are easy to fit at home.

Many enthusiasts fit specialist springs and shock absorbers to cope with the punishment of off-roading, and it is not at all unusual to replace the standard suspension bushes with a plastic set which, some people believe, provide better handling in extreme conditions, along with longer bush life.

Because electric winches impose severe battery drain, even with a high-output alternator running flat-out, it is quite usual to fit a second battery along with a split-charge device. Another option is to replace the standard battery with an Optima spiral-wound type which, with a rating of 850 amps, has enormous reserves of power and can cope with heavy-load, long-running winching operations.

Off-road competition

Anyone wishing to become as proficient as possible in all aspects of off-roading could well consider trying their hand at events like trialling, winching competitions, and other competitive activities which are available through the Land Rover club movement. These are excellent ways to hone off-roading techniques, although in order to take part in many types of competition you need to be fairly proficient in the first place.

Trialling is the logical place to start. Increasing numbers of events are being organised for novice drivers with standard, road-going vehicles. These are often called Tyro or Novice trials, and you can compete in any kind of everyday vehicle. They're classified as RTV (road-taxed vehicle) events.

Most local and regional Land Rover clubs organise a variety of competitions, with beginners' trials becoming ever more popular with recent converts to off-roading. Generally you need to be a club member to take part, although there's often a no-obligation opportunity for first-timers, giving them a chance to try it out before becoming committed to the club world. It's enormous fun,

with masses of help and advice on hand from more experienced enthusiasts.

Provided you understand the basics of off-road driving (such as choosing the right gear, throttle control, reading the way ahead, vehicle placement, etc) and you fully understand the vehicle's controls, you can enjoy events like this without damaging your vehicle or yourself. You'll be certain to improve your skill level in all respects. You'll learn rapidly how to manoeuvre through narrow spaces while at the same time dealing with side

Trials competition is an excellent way to put off-roading skills to the test. There are categories for most types of vehicle, short and long-wheelbases, road-legal (RTV) and competition specials (CCV). (Nick Dimbleby)

slopes, deep holes, rocks, tree roots, and mud; you'll rapidly find out how to choose the most suitable gear for difficult and/or slippery climbs; coping with awkward obstacles will become second nature; and the natural apprehension when driving through water will soon disappear.

One great advantage of trialling – which in itself is a wonderful pastime – is that you can watch how others tackle the same obstacles as yourself. Seeing how fellow competitors manage to make it look easy, or make a complete mess of a section you took in your stride, is a great way to learn.

Once you've got this far you might find yourself developing a healthy interest in winching … enough to start thinking about events like the Warn Challenge. Clearly, winching competitions like this are not for novices – though some clubs organise winching contests suitable for people with limited experience – but even if you don't take part, there's a lot to be learned by watching how more-skilled

enthusiasts do it. To watch a team winch their Land Rover up an impossibly steep hillside, perhaps starting from a muddy river, can be truly inspirational. You'll be given a live demonstration of what so far may have been theory for you: the selection of anchor points; connecting the winch cable to tree strops and ground anchors; effective use of guidance signals; and sensitive control of the winch motor.

It's a big step from being a casual observer to a competitor in something like the Warn Challenge, but the way to do it is to progress through club events until you feel ready for the toughest tests. Obviously, the more demanding winching contests

You have to be pretty serious to become involved in winching competitions such as the Warn Challenge, sponsored by the American Warn organisation. However, it is great fun, despite being exceptionally hard work, usually in terrible conditions. (Nick Dimbleby)

are suitable only for specialised off-road vehicles. Mostly people use 90s fitted with state-of-the-art winches (sometimes with a second one rear-mounted), heavy-duty recovery attachments, mud-terrain tyres, snorkels, and locking differentials.

The ultimate off-roading competition was, at one time, the Camel Trophy. That event is now defunct, and over its last few years had changed into more of an outdoor lifestyle occasion rather than the all-action, driving and winching orientated contest it was in its heyday. Some of the challenges which made the Camel trophy so attractive to Land Rover, as a showcase for its vehicles, crop up in occasional events held in the same style.

Expeditions

Increasingly, European-based Land Rover enthusiasts are stretching their off-roading adventures into parts of north and north-west Africa, heading for the challenges of the Sahara desert and Atlas mountains. Others, even more adventurous, head even further afield.

An expedition to, for example, the Sahara is not something to be undertaken lightly. The environment is always hostile, and can be lethal, and despite the close proximity of the region's northernmost parts to southern Spain, few of the everyday benefits of the 21st century are present. That said, there's no reason why anybody with reasonable off-roading ability and with a Land Rover in good mechanical condition should not head south, cross from Spain to Morocco, and enjoy a bit of real adventure.

It is quite feasible to embark on such a journey with a standard vehicle – after all, the locals manage perfectly well with ordinary cars, many of them seemingly on the verge of extinction. However, they're not planning on living out of their vehicles for weeks on end and, mostly, their desert driving is restricted to established hard-surfaced roads.

A group of two or three enthusiast-driven Land Rovers taking an extended tour around the mountains and deserts of northern Africa can usually manage without major modifications, but deserts are dangerous places, and it's better to be prepared. If you're travelling alone, or intend

venturing into the real wilderness of the region, you must be properly equipped and your vehicle fully suitable for the conditions it will encounter.

The most important pre-expedition check is the cooling system, which has to be able to cope with high-load, slow-speed work in ambient temperatures of 40–45°C, and sometimes more. You may need assistance in the form of a second fan, especially with vehicles more than about five years old, and if you're hitting the Sahara in summer it would be wise to fit one, regardless of the state of the cooling system. Electric fans can be fitted easily to back up the existing one, but

Expeditions can involve everything from desert sands and the worst mud imaginable, to deep snow and impossible ice. A properly prepared vehicle and a well-trained driver can cope with all of these, but only if they have anticipated every eventuality in terms of equipment and expertise. (Nick Dimbleby)

another option is to discard the existing fan altogether and use a pair of smaller ones instead. This will increase the airflow through the radiator, using a larger area of the rad to do so, and thereby giving more cooling efficiency.

A high-level air intake, or snorkel, is a worthwhile fitment for expedition use. There's the obvious benefit of deep wading – remember that flash floods can cause major problems in mountainous areas, even in desert regions – plus the additional benefit of considerably less sand and dust being drawn in when the air intake is at roof height. It means you'll spend less time worrying about the state of the air filter.

If you don't already have one, give serious consideration to a winch. You must have one for solo expeditioning, and at least one vehicle in a group of two or three should be winch-equipped. Choosing one with its own bumper assembly, complete with strong points for a high-lift jack, and specialist towing attachments, saves the bother of adding these separately. But if you don't fit a winch it is essential to have JATE rings fitted to the front of the chassis, and to have a rear tow bar

Part of every off-roader's equipment and an essential item for even modest expeditions, is a high-lift jack. It should be attached so that it can be used without unloading everything, and all members of the party should know how to use it safely. High-lift jacks can be extremely dangerous if used incorrectly. (Nick Dimbleby)

capable of (a) pulling other vehicles and (b) pulling you backwards out of trouble. Make sure the rear crossmember is up to the job.

If your vehicle can't take a high-lift jack, fit the necessary attachments. Nobody should venture into wild country without a high-lift, and careful thought should be given as to where this will be carried, perhaps bolting a mounting system to one rear corner. Make sure it is lockable.

A Land Rover has some vulnerable areas. Hitting a rock with a differential, sump casing, or track rod can leave you stranded hundreds of miles from the nearest town. It therefore pays to fit under-body protection. Most suitable are the large frontal protectors which guard against damage to the steering and the vulnerable front part of the engine sump, and differential guards which should be bolted to the diff casings on both axles.

Headlamps, too, need protection from the stones thrown up by other vehicles on loose-surfaced roads, so fit good lamp guards.

Some arrangement will be needed for carrying extra fuel and drinking water, but there's no need to go to the expense of long-range fuel tanks. Also bear in mind that it's unwise to carry extra fuel inside your vehicle, and that it is illegal to do so in many countries. Instead, invest in a proper expedition roof rack, which will provide a platform for a roof tent as well as secure space for fuel containers.

Don't cut corners on the quality of the roof rack, or on the tent, which ideally should be a proper expedition item. Full-blown expedition roof racks are available from specialist companies, purpose-designed for either 110s or 90s, with special areas for water and fuel containers and a suitable floor for a roof-mounted tent. The same outlets can supply a purpose-designed expedition tent, tailor-made for the roof rack, and constructed in heavy duty cotton canvas, which is the only material suitable for regions such as Africa.

You'll also need to buy or make some window guards to secure partly opened windows, particularly if anybody will be sleeping inside the vehicle. Alternatively, rely on roof vents or sunroof(s) which, with a roof rack over them, provide full security during hot tropical nights.

Work out in advance where heavy items like tool boxes, mechanical spares, and a cooker (with spare gas cylinder) will be stowed, and then bolt some lashing eyes in appropriate positions so that everything can be properly tied down. While planning the interior, bear in mind that a refrigerator will also prove invaluable. Have a look at specialist expedition fridges as well as those sold in caravan and camping outlets, and choose a sensibly sized one which will keep perishable foods fresh and cans of beer cool. Most useful are the type which run on both electricity and gas. Use the Land Rover's electrics during the day, and switch it to gas at night.

Invest in a split-charge twin-battery adaptation; they are inexpensive to install and permit the use of one battery for camp and/or working lamps at night, but leave the main battery untouched for starting power.

Sand ladders are essential and are best carried on the roof, so go for a lightweight type, and devise a locking method for them. The same goes for shovels.

One of the principal items for an overland expedition is an appropriate specialist roof rack, an important use of which is to provide a secure sleeping area, with a suitable canvas expedition tent. It also gives additional storage space. Expedition companies will advise you on the most suitable equipment for individual circumstances, and some will manufacture roof racks to special order. (Nick Dimbleby)

It is possible to extract considerable extra performance from a Tdi or V8 engine. Although this is usually done for road work, high-powered off-roaders are sometimes produced, such as this very special Ninety completed as a special project for Land Rover France, and driven off-road and on-road by the author. (Nick Dimbleby)

may well decide to stick with them.

Be warned that in the desert all non-sand tyres will restrict you to well-used tracks and those areas which you can be sure have a firm surface, and plan your routes accordingly. Attempting deep, soft sand on non-specialist tyres guarantees plenty of practice with sand ladders, shovels, and winches. Tyres with very aggressive treads are often the worst choice.

Better performance

In many ways it seems a little odd to want to turn a Defender into a road-burner, yet there's quite a lot of interest in enhancing the performance of both the petrol V8 and Tdi engines to provide livelier acceleration, higher cruising speeds, and a better maximum.

Specialist companies provide tuning kits for the Tdi engines, consisting of some or all of the following: uprated intercooler, uprated injector pump, alternative turbocharger, modified cylinder head, and sports exhaust. This can make a considerable difference to acceleration, although the 'brick wall' effect of the Defender's shape means that very high maximum speeds are not achievable without a massive improvement in power which is beyond the capability of the 2.5-litre Tdi.

Another popular route to higher performance lies with the 3.9-litre version of the V8 unit, either as a replacement for a Tdi, or with an existing V8 being modified for even more performance. It isn't easy to deal with the electronic management system of the 3.9 when carrying out a DIY engine transplant into a bay which previously held, say, a Tdi. However, it can be done and the results can be startling.

The performance of the V8 can be taken to new heights with a sports cylinder head, sports-profile camshaft, revised induction and exhaust manifolds, and straight-through exhaust system. However, as with the Tdi, the greatest benefit is acceleration. Although maximum speed can be taken beyond 100mph (161kph), there's a massive penalty in fuel consumption to be taken into account because of the Defender's rather pronounced lack of streamlining.

If you can afford it, buy a set of specialist sand tyres, such as Michelin XS. Shod with these, you'll be able to tackle most types of sand (although you're likely to get stuck in deep, loose sand no matter which tyres you use), but sand tyres perform poorly on wet tarmac – so be warned.

If you can't justify sand tyres, your best bet is probably a general-purpose tyre such as the BF Goodrich All-Terrain. You'll need to watch where you go, though, because their ability to get you through soft sand is nowhere near as good as the specialist rubber. Mud-terrain tyres are even less effective in loose sand, but if you already have a set on your vehicle, and they're in good condition, you

Looking after your Land Rover

Because there are nine different engines in the various types of Ninety, One Ten, and Defender, it is not possible in the space available here to provide specific information on routine servicing. However, full details are provided in the relevant Workshop Manuals, the *Haynes Service and Repair Manual* for the series, and the *Haynes Restoration Manual.*

This chapter in no way attempts to replace or even supplement the level of information available in these publications. It comprises, instead, an advisory approach on matters relating to the general care of vehicles in the Defender family. The importance of routine maintenance, and the implications of failure to adhere to service schedules, are spelled out. There's guidance on some of the more usual if not necessarily routine work, and there's an overview of bodywork inspection and renovation.

As well as that, some of the technical concerns associated with ownership of these versatile and complex machines are looked at, from the point of view of the owner who is, perhaps, less experienced than some when it comes to Land Rovers.

Routine maintenance

As with all vehicles, it is crucial to carry out inspection and servicing precisely to the recommended schedules. This applies to all aspects of the vehicle, not just the engine, and in a Land Rover includes steering, transmission, and

A lack of routine oil changes can lead to premature camshaft wear in any engine, but especially Land Rover V8s. This camshaft had developed pronounced early wear because the vehicle's owner neglected servicing requirements. (Dave Barker)

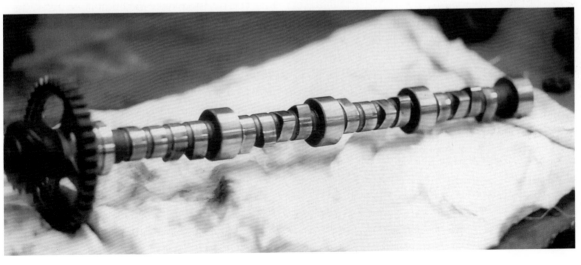

suspension inspection which is not required in some other vehicle types but which, in all of the Defender series, is essential for correct operation.

The V8 petrol engine and the Diesel Turbo and Tdi units are especially sensitive to servicing requirements. If servicing is carried out correctly with high-quality materials the life of these engines will be prolonged considerably.

Particularly susceptible to lax servicing, the V8's working life can be shortened very considerably if oil change intervals are extended or ignored altogether, and/or poor-quality oil is used. The consequential blocked or restricted oilways inhibits the supply of oil to the camshaft and valve gear, leading to premature camshaft wear, noisy and worn hydraulic tappets, and poor running. On the other hand, a V8 which has been treated properly throughout its life can go on to give trouble-free operation over an extremely high mileage.

When ever vehicles are used off-road there is a possibility of damaged or blocked radiators, leading to possible coolant loss and, in the case of mud blockages, almost certain overheating. Aggressive wading risks damage to the radiator from debris in the water unless the grille is covered to protect the delicate radiator behind it. (Dave Barker)

All the turbocharged engines are vulnerable to the effects of infrequent oil changes and inappropriate lubricants. Again, this leads to premature wear, especially in 200 Tdis, which can be prone to crankcase pressurisation because of rapid wear caused by inadequate oil changes. Another result, in all the turbo engines, is premature turbo wear because of oil starvation resulting from partially blocked oilways. It is crucial, too, that coolant levels, radiator performance, and water pump operation are fully up to the mark in all vehicles with these engines.

The V8 produces a great deal of heat which must be properly dispersed if the all-aluminium unit, and particularly the cylinder heads, is not to be damaged. Head gasket problems with the V8 are nearly always caused by under-performing coolant, and it doesn't take long for a blown head gasket to cause serious problems, firstly to the head itself, and also to other areas because of the probable pollution of water with oil, and oil with water.

The coolant level must therefore be checked regularly, and a careful watch maintained on the temperature gauge, especially when operating in hot-weather conditions and/or when towing. As with all modern engines the coolant must be the prescribed mixture of water and antifreeze, which should be checked annually; the use of water alone leads to blocked water channels and does not lubricate the water pump without antifreeze.

The condition of the radiator must be checked after every off-roading expedition. Mud and other debris blocks the airways through the radiator and, if not removed, can lead to extreme overheating in a very short time, with disastrous consequences.

This attention to the cooling system is equally important with Tdi engines. Land Rover diesels are usually very well cooled, which is why a Tdi can be left to tick over for ages without any noticeable increase in coolant temperature, but if anything goes wrong overheating can occur rapidly, again with dire results.

Bodywork renovation

Detailed renovation and restoration advice is provided in the *Haynes Restoration Manual.* It is appropriate here to point out some of the things which go wrong with Land Rovers leading to a need for restoration or, in more extreme cases, replacement.

Front wings are vulnerable on all vehicles, especially so when a Land Rover is used for off-roading. They are easily removed and replaced by anyone with a few basic tools.

The sill strip beneath the doors is extremely vulnerable to off-roading damage, but consists of simple panels held in place with screws and brackets. When replacement becomes necessary it makes sense to consider one of the tough, steel replacement kits specially designed for off-road enthusiasts. These not only resist impact, and therefore retain their appearance, but they also prevent damage to the door bottoms.

Rear doors on Hard Tops and Station Wagons suffer badly from the effects of road dirt, while the hinges wear prematurely because of the substantial weight of the door-mounted spare wheel and tyre. Bolts and hinges can be replaced, or the door can be reskinned or replaced completely. The front and rear side doors suffer badly from the effects of aluminium corrosion through an electrolytic process, and the steel frames rust with equal enthusiasm. The doors are dismantled quite easily and can be replaced partially as required or as complete units

Although the chassis of Land Rovers are extremely durable, they all develop rust with time. Enthusiast-owned vehicles which have regularly been immersed in mud or which have been bounced over rocks will develop chassis rust faster than those which lead a more sheltered life.

While the rear of the chassis is, in some ways, more likely to rust, the front of the vehicle is also vulnerable. Some rust-prone sections, such as the front crossmember, are easy to repair – especially so the crossmember, which is held in place with bolts. Other sections, such as outriggers, will require cutting away before replacements are welded in place. At the same time the area around the outrigger join, along with the entire front-to-rear length of the main chassis frames, should be examined closely and replacement parts welded in as required. The rear crossmember is particularly

The front wings of any vehicle used for off-roading are liable to damage, and the aluminium panels of Land Rovers are virtually impossible to panel beat back into shape. Replacement sections are easy to fit, and are not expensive. (Dave Barker)

vulnerable to rust and, because it carries all the stresses of towing, must be checked with particular care, along with the ends of the chassis rails to which it attaches. When replacing, always use a

The sill panels of 90s and 110s are vulnerable to damage from rocks, earth banks and tree debris. Sill protectors, like this one fitted to a 90, bolt to the chassis and protect the lower door area, as well as retaining the good looks of the sill area, even after heavy-duty off-roading. (Dave Barker)

The best position for the spare wheel and tyre is on the rear door, although the extra weight leads to premature wear of the door hinges. Fortunately, they are not difficult or expensive to replace. (Dave Barker)

crossmember with extension legs which fit over the ends of the chassis to ensure the strongest possible repair.

Brakes

Replacement of brake pads for front and rear (where discs are fitted) is straightforward and won't cause any problems to anyone who has carried out such work on other vehicles. One important point to remember is that shims might be fitted to the rear of the brake pads. If so, make sure the right shims go back in the right place. Another point to bear in mind is that split pins are used to secure the caliper retaining pins, and new split pins must be fitted whenever removal has been necessary.

The front brake caliper can be removed, perhaps for work on the front suspension, without disturbing the hydraulic connections. Alternatively, it can be taken off the vehicle altogether. Rear calipers (where used) do not have a flexible hose, so cannot be removed without disturbing the hydraulic system. Models prior to 1994 were fitted with rear drum brakes, and although shoe replacement is a more protracted job than fitting pads to a disc system, there's nothing particularly difficult about it. The important thing, especially if you're not doing this sort of job every day, is never to attempt to rush any work on the braking system.

Non-routine mechanical work

Neither spring nor shock absorber replacement requires any special skills and, to be fair, neither does much of the work you might need to do on the steering linkage, suspension joints, anti-roll bar bushes, and so on. However, there are jobs which are much more difficult and not for the novice, unless there's someone to help (despite the

The rear crossmember takes all the stresses of towing and must therefore be rust free, other than perhaps the inevitable surface blemishing. The tow hitch assembly should also be inspected carefully on a regular basis. (Dave Barker)

There's nothing complicated about the front disc brakes used on Defenders, although some have shims fitted behind the pads, which must be replaced with care when renewing pads. (Dave Barker)

excellence of Workshop Manuals). This includes engine removal and stripdown, gearbox removal, clutch work, steering box and front swivel pin assembly replacement or overhaul, and front and rear hub overhaul and replacement.

Technical topics

Fuel savers

The heavy fuel consumption of all Land Rovers is a worry to many owners who find their vehicles more expensive to run than they had expected. Naturally, the V8-powered models are the worst offenders, but some people also become concerned with the amount of diesel consumed by Tdis, the most efficient of all Land Rover diesels other than the much newer TD5.

Too many owners who are new to Land Rovers fail to check out the likely fuel consumption before they take the plunge for the first time. It should be obvious that anything weighing two tons or more, with appalling aerodynamics, complex and energy-sapping transmission and, more often than not, off-roading tyres, will not be cheap to run. In all cases the burden can be eased slightly, but it must be remembered that a 90 or 110 simply cannot be as economical as a Discovery or Range Rover fitted with the same engine.

The worst fuel consumption of all is found with early One Tens fitted with the 3.5-litre petrol engine and four-speed gearbox. It is just a little better with later One Tens, which had five-speed transmission, and with all V8 Ninetys, which had five gears. The best consumption you can expect with early One Tens is 13–15mpg, but even later versions and Ninetys will rarely, if ever, return better than 14–17mpg.

In order to get the best possible fuel consumption from the thirsty V8 everything must be in top order. Spark plugs need to be changed at the recommended intervals to avoid them ending up like this, causing poor starting, and raising fuel consumption. (Dave Barker)

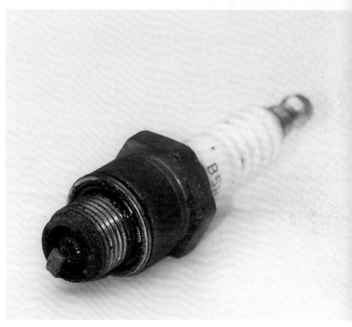

The turbocharger must always be functioning correctly. Wear is inevitable over high mileages, especially where oil changes have been neglected. Reconditioned units are less expensive than new replacements and perform equally well. (Dave Barker)

So what can be done?

Firstly, all Land Rover V8s will run on unleaded fuel without difficulty, and usually without adjustment of the ignition timing. Many owners mistakenly believed in the past that four-star was necessary – sometimes because they had been misinformed when buying – and in these non-four-star days some owners are even using lead replacement fuel additives. This is not necessary.

An electric cooling fan instead of the standard viscous-coupled unit provides a very slight saving, while synthetic lubricants in the engine and transmission can reduce drag. However, you've got to be doing a high mileage in order to achieve any financial benefits with these.

Swapping those mean-looking mud-terrain tyres for road-bias rubber is worth doing if you spend all your time on tarmac, but not if you enjoy off-roading.

But there are actions you can take which cost very little and which will optimise consumption. Spark plugs need to be in perfect condition, the distributor and the rest of the ignition system must be functioning at full efficiency, timing must be spot-on, the air filter clean, and the carburettors checked for wear and leaks, and properly balanced. Replacing an early standard ignition with an electronic system, such as Lumenition, can itself improve consumption by at least 1mpg, which is worth doing when the base figure is about 14mpg.

There's less you can do with diesels, and even the Tdi engine can produce a consumption figure no better than 22–23mpg when worked hard in a Defender, improving to a very best of perhaps 28mpg on a long journey. On average, a Tdi will give somewhere between 24 and 27mpg.

It is crucial with diesels to ensure that the injectors are functioning at 100 per cent efficiency, with spot-on timing and no defects in the pump. This can only be checked and, if necessary, set up with professional equipment, but is worth doing from time to time.

With the Diesel Turbo and 200 and 300 Tdi it's vital that the turbocharger is functioning correctly and that waste gate and pressure sensing lines are not contaminated with oil. Air leaks sometimes occur with turbochargers and it's inevitable that, with time, the turbo will develop problems, resulting in a very noticeable performance drop and an increase in fuel consumption. Turbochargers cannot be repaired at home, but various specialist companies provide exchange renovation schemes at a lower cost than a new unit. Intercooler problems with Tdis can also have a marked effect on consumption and performance.

Defender overdrive

Another tried and tested way of improving fuel consumption is to fit an overdrive, popular with owners of earlier Land Rovers and a wide range of classic cars but, until recently, not an option for the Defender owner. An overdrive unit built by GKN Driveline and available through a limited number of UK specialists now makes it possible for owners of five-speed Defenders to increase substantially the overall gearing of their vehicles.

The unit bolts directly to the LT230 transfer box and is compatible with the LT77 and R380 gearboxes. It reduces engine revs by 28.3 per cent and can produce a 20 per cent saving in fuel, depending on type of use. It is most beneficial in Defenders which are used regularly for long road journeys when, as well as the fuel saving, the reduction in mechanical noise because of the reduced engine speed makes a significant difference to overall comfort levels. The cost on introduction in 1999 was about £1,000 including VAT. Anybody regularly using a Defender for long-distance travel would soon recoup this.

The GKN overdrive is fitted through the floor by removing the centre seat. The job is straightforward and can be accomplished without special mechanical knowledge or equipment. Selection is via a button switch on the gear knob which activates the unit's hydraulic operating system, giving a smooth and positive shift into or out of overdrive. It defaults to direct drive in the event of a problem with the electrical or hydraulic systems.

It's a tough, long-lasting fitment easily capable of withstanding the heavy use to which many Defenders are subjected. Supplying agents provide a full back-up service.

Get converted

A third way of reducing fuel costs with 2.5-litre and 3.5-litre petrol vehicles is to have them converted to LPG. The conversion gives virtually the same economy and performance from a fuel which is roughly half the price of petrol. Other advantages include full dual-fuel capability, which enables you to continue using petrol whenever necessary and, with both gas and petrol tanks full, a much extended range. There are also disadvantages, however. The large LPG tank inhibits the load-carrying capability of a 90, although it's much less of a problem with a 110, and LPG refuelling centres are still difficult to find in some areas, especially out of normal working hours.

The cost of conversion varies and it pays to get at least a couple of quotes before going ahead. And bear in mind that a little-used Land Rover, even with a V8 engine, would probably take several years to repay the cost of conversion. For high-mileage users it's nevertheless attractive on a cost basis, provided the availability problem can be overcome.

Transfer swap

Gearbox conversions are less common than engine transplants, and transfer box conversions even more so. However, one way of raising the overall gearing of, say, a Ninety fitted with the 2.5-litre petrol engine is to replace the standard transfer

The cost of running a V8 can be reduced by roughly 50 per cent by investing in an LPG conversion, although low mileage users will take some time to recover the cost. This is a belly tank for the LPG, fitted under the driver's door. (Dave Barker)

box with one from a Discovery or pre-viscous coupled Range Rover. This raises the gearing by about 15 per cent, which provides a small boost to fuel economy and makes cruising a little more restful. However, anyone considering this should not do so if larger diameter tyres are already fitted, and should not fit larger tyres afterwards, because this would make the gearing uncomfortably high for the engine and considerably reduce the ability to make full use of fifth gear. Nor is it an option if the Land Rover is to be used heavily loaded, or if any towing is contemplated.

The conversion itself is straightforward, although two holes will be needed for the handbrake brackets. These should be drilled and tapped before the transfer box is installed.

Another conversion which can be carried out is with the Borg-Warner chain-driven unit from later Range Rover classics. However, the dimensions are

different and the unit will not fit straight in without a certain amount of modification beneath the vehicle. But almost anything is possible with Land Rovers!

Spare wheel tips

The factory-fitted standard spare wheel position for members of the Defender family is on the rear door. This doesn't suit everybody and there's always the problem that the considerable weight of the wheel and tyre causes premature wear of the door hinges. There's only one approved alternative mounting position, but one or two other methods of carrying the spare are worth considering.

Anyone not wishing to use the rear door to carry the spare, for whatever reason, can buy a bonnet mounting kit. There are drawbacks, however, because a bonnet-mounted spare inhibits forward visibility, particularly in some off-roading situations, such as when cresting a steep hill. The weight of the spare also makes it difficult to lift the bonnet, and requires the use of a sturdy additional prop (a length of timber or steel) to ensure it won't accidentally fall on you when you're working

An alternative to the rear door position for the spare wheel is to use a bonnet mounting kit. However, the wheel and tyre impairs vision, especially when driving off-road, and makes the bonnet extremely heavy to lift. (Dave Barker)

beneath it. Furthermore, the weight causes extra wear of the bonnet hinges and release mechanism, especially with regular off-roading.

Other positions worth considering include inside the vehicle, if you don't need the space, or on an expedition-style roof rack if you're strong enough to lift it up there and get it down when required.

It's not unknown for previous owners to have removed the rear door mounting components, perhaps when using an alternative position. The parts can be obtained as a complete kit from Land Rover dealers, or you can use one of the swing-away kits sold by a number of accessory specialists.

Smoke signals

Among the many myths about Land Rover engines is that they are bound to smoke, and that the normally aspirated diesel engines are sure to smoke more than petrol units. However, this isn't an across-the-board statement of truth because there is always a reason for engines to produce smoke. Older units are more inclined to smoke, of course, but there's still a reason behind the annoying habit.

So, to dispel one belief, diesel engines (normally aspirated or turbocharged) do not produce, as a breed, any more smoke than their petrol-fuelled counterparts. Their fumes can be more visible, and it is the colour of the smoke which gives the strongest clues as to their cause.

The majority of higher-mileage diesel engines will puff a little black smoke when starting from cold. However, if it's more than a modest mini-cloud it suggests that the injectors are either worn or badly adjusted. The good news is that they are easily removed for replacement or servicing.

If the smoke is white the cause is almost certainly an excess of fuel, which is usually due to problems with the distributor pump, or its timing.

When you see blue or blue-tinged smoke on start-up or when accelerating after being on over-run, it is most probably caused by wear in the valve guides and seals (see the section on start-up smoke below). If blue smoke doesn't disappear from the exhaust after start-up and persists while you're driving, it's almost certain you have wear in the bores and that the pistons and piston rings

have also developed serious wear. There may even be broken piston rings.

The most serious of these problems is cylinder wear. To check for it, remove the engine breather cap while the unit is running and then slowly increase the revs. If the bores, pistons, and rings are worn beyond normal tolerances they will allow the crankcase to pressurise, blowing oil mist or smoke out of the cap. And if that happens you're facing a major stripdown.

Start-up smoke

Owners of older Land Rovers have always accepted a large puff of smoke when starting the engine as something to expect. If this happens with a more modern vehicle it can be worrying, especially to those with limited mechanical knowledge. Of course, the more modern engines used in Ninetys

Despite what some people might tell you, Land Rover engines are not designed to smoke! Very often, smoke from the exhaust on startup is caused by wear in the valve stem oil seals which, while not a serious problem, will require rectification in time. (Dave Barker)

and One Tens (except for the four-cylinder petrol and normally aspirated diesel units) do not usually smoke unless there is something seriously wrong with them. Or do they?

Any engine which has done more than about 80,000 miles (129,000km) can develop start-up smoking, and this does not necessarily mean a major overhaul is due, a breakdown is rapidly heading your way, or MOT failure is imminent. In most cases, the smoke is caused by nothing more serious than worn valve stem seals. When these seals have become worn they allow a small amount of oil to drop down from the rockers when the engine is stationary, past the seal, and down to the back of the valves. The moment you start the

Even a dense, black cloud does not necessarily mean serious trouble. It can mean the engine is being 'over-fuelled', signifying a problem with the injector pump, the timing or the injectors, or perhaps all three. If there is no reliable record of the cambelt of a Tdi engine having been changed recently, it is essential to do this immediately after buying. The better specialist dealers will do it as a matter of course when preparing a vehicle for its new owner. This shows the cambelt arrangement in the 300 Tdi. (Dave Barker)

engine this oil is burnt off and produces a smoke cloud.

This wear can develop without you being aware of it, but will gradually get worse until the oil seals have to be replaced. This usually involves cylinder head removal, which is not particularly complicated, although there's obviously more to it with the twin heads of the V8 engine.

Cambelt dilemma

Whenever buying a used diesel-engined Land Rover – no matter whether it's a pre-Tdi 2.5-litre engine or a 200 or 300 Tdi – it's essential to examine the service history closely, if there is one. The history will help you decide whether or not to proceed with the purchase: the more complete the service story, the more faith you can have in the vehicle's mechanical side.

One aspect to be looked for above all others, once you have actually decided to go ahead, is information relating to cambelt changes. If there's any uncertainty at all, and especially if there is no service history, budget for a belt replacement before you begin using the Land Rover.

If a cambelt has gone beyond its recommended

replacement point it will be worn, and could fail at any time. You get no warning of failure; one moment the engine's running perfectly and the next it's stopped, often with a loud bang. A broken belt invariably means some degree of engine damage, which can be severe – so don't risk it.

You don't have the same problem with V8s, of course, because they have chain drive for the single camshaft. With these engines it's essential to listen for a front-end rattling noise, which indicates a worn chain. Although V8 timing chains will continue to run with a rattle, sometimes for years, any appreciable increase in noise means that replacement is due.

Brake problems

The brakes of Defenders which are used regularly off-road, especially where deep mud is involved, can wear faster than usual, and sometimes unevenly, even though the vehicle may not do too much road driving. The cause is the abrasiveness of some of the stuff the vehicle gets immersed in, pistons and pads 'sticking' because of mud, and the devastation caused to any moving parts whenever sand is driven through. Front brakes are particularly vulnerable, and sometimes there can be considerable variation in the wear rate of the front pads.

A difference of 5mm or more in the friction material qualifies as an excessive difference in pad wear rate. As well as the 'sticking' of pads and pistons, this can also be caused by a badly worn or rough disc surface on the side of the worst-worn pad (which can result from off-roading). Inferior quality pads can also have uneven wear rates.

The state of the discs is easily checked simply by looking at them. If there's any deep scoring – often caused by off-roading – or corrosion, or the disc is unevenly worn in any way at all, the only cure is to fit new discs. As with the replacement of brake pads, discs should only ever be replaced as a pair.

Correct operation of the piston can be checked by removing the normally worn pad and getting an assistant to gently apply the footbrake so that the pistons can be seen to emerge equally and steadily from the caliper. Take great care with this, though, because if you overdo it the piston could pop out of the bore.

One of the worst enemies of any Land Rover used for off-roading is accumulated mud and sand around the underside of the vehicle. Always power wash thoroughly after off-road outings, getting the water into all the hidden areas and the awkward upper sections of the chassis. Do not forget to blast away at the brakes in order to clean muck away from discs and calipers. (Dave Barker)

After 'opening' the pistons, retract them using a lever or a pair of grips, checking that the resistance felt from each one appears to be equal. If it's not, the caliper must be checked professionally, or you may decide to simply invest in a new one.

Finally, never buy cheap or unknown brake components. Uneven wear is one thing, but pad break-up or some other failure could lead to total loss of braking.

Because off-roading is unkind to brakes and other components, the underside of the vehicle should be power-washed after every session, including the brakes, which should be inspected carefully on a very regular basis. It is not enough to rely on the normal service schedules.

Appendix

Off-road centres, clubs, and vehicle sales

A comprehensive list of off-road training and experience centres is given in the *Off-Road 4-Wheel Drive Book* by Jack Jackson, also published by Haynes. Some of the larger centres advertise regularly in Land Rover magazines. Full listings are published from time to time.

There are too many Land Rover clubs to list here. Because details change regularly, reference should be made to specialist magazines, which usually print fully up-to-date listings.

For companies specialising in the sale of Land Rovers and for up-to-date price information it is advisable to check the Land Rover press, particularly for ex-military vehicles, plus the various mart-style publications.

Specialists

Among the suppliers of some of the items specifically referred to in this book are the following:

Reference books
LRE Bookshop, 01379 890111. Full range of Land Rover books, manuals, catalogues, handbooks, and videos.

Models
Landcraft, 01678 520820. The world's largest range of Land Rover models.

Roll cages
Safety Devices roll cages are available through numerous stockists. For details and brochure, telephone 01353 724201, or fax 01353 724213.
Arrow Services, 01302 341154.
Bettaweld, 01302 351264.
Frogs Island 4x4, 01491 824020.
Mantec Services, 02476 395368.
Nene Overland, 01733 380687.
Rogers of Bedford, 01234 348469.
Roll Centre, 01480 464052.
Scorpion Racing, 020 7485 5581.
Simmonites, 01274 833351.

Electric fans
Kenlowe, 01628 823303.
Merlin Motorsport (for Tripac fans), 01249 782101.
Pacet, 01628 526754.

Locking differentials
Ashcroft Transmissions, 01582 750400.
Frogs Island 4x4, 01491 824020.
Warwick 4x4, 01926 864404.

Hydraulic winches
Milemarker, 01460 61674.

Tdi performance equipment
Gratech, 01621 842020.

GKN Overdrive
Ashcroft Transmissions, 01582 750400.
Frogs Island 4x4, 01491 824020.
GKN Driveline, 0121 313 1661.
Warwick 4x4, 01926 864404.

Land Rover insurance

Admiral, 0800 600 800.

Adrian Flux, 01553 777888.

Firebond, 07000 347326.

4x4 Insurance Direct, 01829 733880.

Heritage, 0121 246 6060.

Lancaster, 01480 484848.

NFU Mutual, 01829 771066.

Peter Best, 01621 840400.

Privilege, 0870 243 5555.

Secure Direct, 0500 417270.

Snowball, 0870 742 5202.

Sureterm Direct, 0700 2020230.

General suppliers

Anchor Supplies, 01773 570137. Ex-military tents and equipment.

APB Trading, 01299 250174. General and specialist spares and accessories.

Arrow Services, 01302 341154. Parts, accessories, tyres, servicing and chassis replacement.

Autopost, 0208 675 4022. Spares and accessories; worldwide mail order.

Bettaweld, 01724 798691. Roof racks, protective bars, etc.

BJ Acoustics, 0161 627 0873. Sound reduction materials.

BLRS, 0121 373 7425. General parts, chassis, exhausts, accessories, seats, and trim.

Brownchurch, 020 8556 0011. Expedition equipment and tent specialist.

Chris Perfect Components, 01570 423206. Disc brakes for Series Land Rovers, parabolic springs, etc.

Coverall Europe, 01943 879111. Seat cover specialist.

Dakar Cars, 01322 614044. General and specialist parts, body conversions and LPG conversions.

David Bowyer's Off-Road Centre, 01363 82666. Winches and specialist recovery equipment; winch servicing.

Designa Chassis, 01302 341153. Replacement chassis, coil-spring conversion chassis, special parts fabricator.

Dingocraft, 01494 448367. Diesel timing kits, Lumenition ignition kits, suspension bushes.

DLS, 01629 822185. Personal and mail order parts and accessories; vehicle servicing and bodywork.

Dunsfold Land Rover, 01483 200567. Early parts specialist, repairs, conversions. Home of the Dunsfold Land Rover collection.

Equicar, 01902 882883. Second-hand engines and gearboxes.

Famous Four, 01507 609444. Suspension specialists, general parts and equipment.

Frogs Island 4x4, 01491 824020. Specialist off-road and performance parts, equipment and conversions.

Gratech, 01621 842020. Full range of parts and equipment. Specialist performance conversions for Tdis.

Home Guard, 01832 734630. Military clothing, tents, outdoor equipment.

Intamech Power Drive, 01384 413413. Sole importer for Warn Winches, Black Diamond, and Hi-Lift specialist off-road accessories.

John Craddock, 01543 577207. Personal and worldwide mail order parts and accessories, wheels, tyres, and ex-military vehicles.

LEGS, 01691 653737. Specialist engine and gearbox reconditioning.

LR Supermarket, 0151 486 8636. Genuine Land Rover accessories specialist.

Machine Mart, 0115 956 5555. General and workshop tools, welding equipment, compressors, etc.

Mantec Services, 02476 395368. Expedition equipment and clothing, off-road accessories and equipment, roll cages.

Martin Motors, 01905 451506. Range Rover parts and accessories specialist.

Motor Climate UK, 0121 766 5006. Air conditioning, cruise control, etc.

Motor & Diesel Engineering, 01954 719549. Tdi performance conversions, replacement diesels, LPG conversion.

Nationwide Trim, 01527 518851. Interior trim and seating specialist.

Nene Valley Off-Road, 01604 781187. Wheel and tyre specialist.

North Staffs 4x4, 01785 811211. General and specialist parts, equipment and services.

Oxted Trimming, 01883 717038. Specialist seat trim for all Land Rovers.

Paddock, 01629 584499. General and specialist parts and accessories; worldwide mail order.

PRB Services, 0113 279 6039. Parts from dismantled vehicles.

Rimmer Bros, 01522 568000. Stainless steel exhaust systems.

RK Automotive, 01827 63866. Components, engines, parts, vehicles, gas conversions.

Ryders International, 0151 933 4338. Winches and off-road accessories and equipment.

Scorpion Racing, 020 7485 5581. Competition equipment specialist.

Servicetune, 0161 799 8543. Wing protectors, steering guards, wing sections, door parts.

Simmonites, 01274 83351. Specialist off-road equipment, general parts and accessories, tyres, vehicles.

Southam Tyres, 01926 813888. Off-road and general 4x4 tyres specialist.

Steve Parker, 01706 854222. Off-road and conversion equipment, specialist parts and equipment.

Sunrise Electronics, 020 7637 3727. GPS equipment specialist.

Terrain Master, 01206 391350. Recovery and protection equipment.

Trakkers, 01564 777 232. Replacement seats, extra seats, cubby boxes, trim.

UK Wire & Rope, 01223 294156. Ropes, shackles, blocks for all recovery purposes.

Warwick 4x4, 01926 864404. All aspects of vehicle engineering, refurbishment and upgrading.

West Coast Off-Road, 01704 229014. Wheel and tyre specialist.

Index